How to Make, Market and Sell Ebooks All for Free

Ebooksuccess4free

Jason Matthews

Truckee, California. USA

ISBN: 1451537077
EAN-13: 9781451537079

Also by Jason Matthews

The Little Universe - a novel

Jim's Life - the sequel novel

Get On Google Front Page

How to Make Your Own Free Website: And Your Free Blog Too

This book is dedicated to three beautiful ladies.

For Jana, Shelby and Devan;

I love each of you very much.

Table of Contents:

Introduction   1
The Wrong Ways to Spend Your Money   5
Ebooks versus Paper or DTB (dead tree books)   12
Social Media   15
Deciding on a Domain Name   32
Creating Your Blog Site   38
Cover Design   48
Formatting and Uploading for Smashwords, Amazon and
other Retailers   56
Formatting for Your Sites, Making Your own Conversions 72
Creating Your Website   80
SEO (Search Engine Optimization)   89
Preparing Your Website for Ebook Sales   99
Selling Your Ebook from Your Websites   106
PR (Public Relations)   124
Reviews and Critiques   129
Affiliate Marketing   133
Other Things You Can Do   136
Maintenance   145
Addendum/Amendments/Additions   148
Review List of Highly Recommended Programs and Sites 149
Organizations to Donate to Once You Can   151
Cheating With Money   152

Introduction

Okay, you've written a book or are in the process of writing one. Congratulations! I don't say that lightly either. As an author of five books, two of which are full length novels, I know writing a book can be extremely challenging, especially if you've put the effort and dedication into writing a *great* book and not just a bunch of fluff on pages.

But what next; what do you do once it's written? Have you heard the saying, that writing the book is half the battle while marketing it is the other half? When I first heard this comment, I was nearly finished writing my first novel. I thought, *that's crazy because writing this book has taken me years. No way can marketing it be as difficult.* Unfortunately I was in for a surprise in the form of a hard lesson as they usually seem to be in my life. Advice like this came and I thought, *yeah, maybe for someone else, but mine will be a success right out of the gates because my book is really good.*

And I still believe success is coming. It's just the "right out of the gates" part I've come to realize was painfully inaccurate. Many of us like to think our words are golden and when we finish writing our books, our certain best-sellers, that they're going to fly directly from our hands into the eyes of readers around the globe. Agents and publishers will beat a path to our door to whisk us off our feet with huge advances, offers for sequels and world tour book signings. Movie producers will fight over the rights to make the next Oscar winning best picture. We may even imagine what we'll wear on the red carpet at Oscar night and how our award speech will go... thanking the little people... the tear-filled pause... etc.

It's a great dream, one that I've been dreaming for several years. I haven't given up on the ultimate goals of the dream, but I have *altered my timeframe* for all of this to happen. It came not by choice but out of necessity.

And please know this; I'm not here to squash anyone's dream. In fact, just the opposite. I encourage everyone to dream big. Hopefully your book, or books, will be tremendously successful and touch the lives of millions of readers. *What I am here to do is share what I've learned along the way,* advice that will save you vast amounts of time, money and frustration and also help you avoid many of the costly mistakes that I made after finishing my first novel. Because I found out the hard way there are dozens of things that could have been done FOR FREE that would have been more effective for marketing and selling my books than the things I did.

(Side note; this advice is not about how to write a book. I'm assuming you've already done that or are nearly finished. This is about what comes next and how to maximize results with minimal effort in the shortest time frame with the least amount of money from your pocket.)

Let me share a little background about my experience.

Back in 1990 I graduated from the University of North Carolina with a degree in RTVMP (Radio, Television and Motion Picture). I moved to Los Angeles and got some entry level jobs at film industry companies. The jobs weren't exciting. I mostly drove around the LA highways as an errand runner or PA (Production Assistant) and cursed at the congestion of traffic.

Like so many people in LA, I also wrote a screenplay on the side. I believed my idea was terrific, and if I could just finish my screenplay and get it into the hands of the right person, **voila,** everything would fall into place.

2

Of course it didn't happen that way. After a year of constantly driving, my car's engine died. I then lost my job, went broke and left LA for the mountains of Lake Tahoe to become a ski-bum and re-evaluate my life mission. When I wasn't skiing I worked as a snowmaker in the winter and a house painter in the summer. On the side I managed to finish that screenplay but trying to find an agent from Tahoe wasn't easy, especially before the internet, and the agent I signed with probably had little to no real connections.

Years passed. Nothing happened. I got very good at skiing and painting houses, but my story just existed in some pages on my shelf and in my head. My agent disappeared.

More years passed. By 2000, a voice from within started screaming, *hey, you've still got to write this story and get the movie made!* I knew it was correct but didn't know what to do. Fortunately, I'd read a few books that had great story lines but were poorly written. The crazy thing was that they became best-sellers. It made me think I could do it too.

Near the end of 2000 I began writing the novel version of my screenplay. I worked with it on and off, sometimes being diligent and sometimes not. It took several years, but I eventually wrote a full length novel and people liked it. Originally it was called *The Big Bang: Notes from Looking Within*. Not wanting to repeat the hassle of agents and publishers, I self-published it POD style (Print On Demand) in September of 2005. The title changed to *The Little Universe* and I also began writing the sequel, *Jim's Life*.

Looking back on the past five years, I did two things for my writing career. I wrote a second novel and marketed the first one in all the worst ways possible. It was so easy to spend thousands of dollars on things that sounded good but just didn't work.

Recently after finishing the sequel I realized a great truth. There was no way I could afford to market my books anymore with expensive ideas and no guarantee that they'd work. I made a firm decision for promoting the sequel. This was the concept;

3

The Wrong Ways to Spend Your Money

The following is a list of things I tried that either didn't work or were not cost effective. There are plenty of ideas I haven't tried, but anything that requires a fair amount of money with no guarantee can go here too.

Printing and Shipping.

I spent hundreds of dollars each year printing copies of my screenplay and then novel and sending them to agents and publishers. Each copy cost around $12 to $15 to make, plus the shipping to get it there and the SASE (Self-Addressed Stamped Envelope) to return it when they eventually would. So each package totaled close to $20 with the shipping, and I felt bad knowing I cost at least one large tree its life with all that wasted paper. Months later I'd invariably get my work returned with a note from the agency/publisher that read something like this;

Thank you for your interest in our agency/publishing house. We have reviewed your materials and determined that it doesn't meet the criteria of what we're presently looking for. We wish you the best of luck in your endeavors as we know how nearly impossible it is to get published. Hahahahaha.

Of course I've embellished on the ha-ha-ha part as they were always polite, but that's how it felt at the post office after reading those rejection letters that were probably mailed by the same twenty-year old intern who passed on my novel. (Clearly not bitter about it, am I?)

Print On Demand (POD) Publishing.

I went with Authorhouse. They were the biggest outfit and really sucked me in. I went with a fairly extensive package of bells and whistles, including the editing and some of the marketing services. I spent around $3,200 just to get my initial run of 100 paperback books made. After that I could order more paperbacks for around $9/apiece for print runs of 200 copies or more. Knowing the book would only sell for perhaps $15, I soon realized this was going to be an extremely difficult way to earn any real money. And coupled with the fact that I gave away so many free copies for reviews in the hope that new readers would generate more readers and someday orders, I sold far fewer than needed to turn any profit.

The other bad thing about POD publishing, and this is the part the companies don't tell you, is that *large book stores don't buy POD books*. They just don't. It's like an unwritten rule. If you get one of their buyers on the phone, they'll tell you it's because they can't get them at a 40% discount rate; instead it's just 35%. But there's more to it. Large publishing houses spend big bucks on advertising, including location. Location is everything in book stores, and the big publishers pay to make sure their books, and not those of POD or independent authors, will have the best shelf display and placements.

My advice is to stay away from POD unless you absolutely must have some print copies made. And if you do, do it for free (CreateSpace). We'll get to more on that in a later section.

Webdesigners.

I spent thousands of dollars on two different professional webdesigners. In each case they did their best to interpret my concepts and come up with websites that worked for me. But ultimately the pages did little to advance my career and book sales, plus I could have created them myself for free. I just didn't know that back then. Had I known how easy it was to create my own websites for free, it would have saved massive amounts of time, money and frustration. And the other thing about hiring a webdesigner is the wait. Often it takes days or even weeks to get a few simple words changed or added. Imagine not wanting to email your designer and ask them to add a paragraph because the last time they did something like that it took six days and cost $50.

Advertising.

It's easy to spend huge dollars on advertising whether it's radio, TV, magazines, newspapers or Pay per Click options. To get any kind of decent coverage, the amounts they'll demand will be outrageous and the results won't have any guarantee whatsoever. I ran a radio ad that broadcasted in my hometown and beyond for about $500 which aired a few times a day for three months. That resulted in a couple of sales. I also ran a small magazine ad for about $100 that I believe added up to zero sales. I tried a bit of Pay per Click through Google AdWords but mostly just watched the initial deposit quickly vanish to zero. Plus it would have been easy to spend much more on major newspaper or magazine ads. The simple fact of advertising this way is that it's grossly expensive and probably only makes sense with a book that is already successful and known.

Book Stores.

Another of my horrible ideas was to send free copies of my novel to bookstores across America. I figured someone there would read my book, realize it was good, start selling it and order more copies. So I researched bookstores across the states and mailed 150 copies at costs to me of $9 apiece plus a few dollars for shipping. I spent close to $2,000 on this half-baked idea. Did any of these book stores ever contact me for more books? Nope, not

7

one. Did a bunch of copies show up for sale on Amazon for one penny? Yep, a huge number of them. The rest probably either got sold at a major discount or simply thrown away. It makes me sad to think how many of my books have been tossed in the garbage, and yet it was entirely my fault for not going about things smarter. In hindsight, if I had just called these bookstores and talked with the person in charge of purchases, I would have found out either to not send the book or how to have done so properly.

However, that being said, bookstores are still terrible places for new authors to sell books in amounts that really matter. They place your book deep in a shelf, spine out, and sell maybe a few copies every couple of months. Then you have to track them down with the invoice and get your check, an amount that you realize was barely even worth it. My advice (if you end up having physical books) is to stay away from bookstores until they order from you and pay up front.

Conferences.

This is one that I have mixed feelings about because you can make some really valuable contacts, have good experiences and get information from conferences, but you will spend loads of money along the way. I probably didn't say that with enough emphasis so let me repeat; *you will spend LOADS of money at conferences.* I've done four, and each time I not only paid for the conference but I paid for the travel and the hotel stay. Take all the costs into consideration: conference, products, hotel room, travel, parking, eating out, extras, baby sitters, etc. When it added up, I spent a minimum of $1,200 at the least expensive one and around $4,000 at the most. On average each conference, with all the total costs added up, ran close to $2,000.

(Side note; at this point you might be asking how I could afford this? I couldn't really. I was using up all the money I ever made as a house painting contractor, plus I took out a second mortgage on my house to borrow up to $100,000 so I could

8

continue blowing it on bad marketing ideas. I naively used credit to market my book.)

Back to conferences. I say don't do them unless you have a darned good reason for being there and can do it on the cheap. It will help if you can stay at home or with friends in the area. You should also be extremely prepared to make the most of it, as in having your work finely polished, researching the top people that will be there and the workshops and how to do it to the fullest. Otherwise, save your money.

I've done plenty of other things that didn't pan out. I spent money on a part-time marketing person. She didn't do much except give advice like where to advertise and which conferences to attend. She also told me to submit my book to Oprah. *Great idea! I'll bet nobody's thought of that, and Oprah is just dying to have a suggestion for a new book.* I also spent $800 on stickers and gave them away and stuck them to things wherever I went. That was kind of a cool idea but far too much money. I don't think it sold any books, but everyone likes stickers and I still give them to random kids that come over.

The point is, I spent money for years and none of that worked. When I finished writing a second novel I vowed not to do anything that wasn't free. And so I didn't. I stuck to just doing free things, and the results have been remarkable. I'm selling more books than ever before, and guess what it's costing? Zilch. Nada. Nothing.

And now, I'd like to tell you the absolutely 100% free things you can do that are also 100% guaranteed not to waste any money. *And if you do them and do them well, you will sell books.* It's up to you. Do you want to sell books on a budget that everyone can afford? I promise this much; if you follow these tips **you will only invest your time.** It won't cost one penny. You have nothing to lose and everything to gain.

The following chapters are all the things you can do right away to make, market and sell your book for free.

But before we get to that, let me mention two things. First, the order in which you do the coming tips is not mandatory to follow. You can do them in several orders and still succeed. This is just my recommendation, what I've found from experience to make the most sense. Some of you may not need much advice on social marketing or blog creation, for examples, and so you may want to skim those parts. I also recommend you read through this entirely before getting entrenched in any one area. Then you'll have a clearer idea on the whole scheme of things when you get started. Or, you can actually follow these steps like a manual and it will still work just fine. The order is really up to you.

Secondly, I'm going to present you with a wealth of information. For some, much of this will be new; for others there will be parts that feel like a review. All of it has to do with online methods for accomplishing your goals so those who are less familiar with the internet and their computers may at times feel overwhelmed. Not to worry, *feeling overwhelmed by this is a natural response and something I've also experienced plenty of times.* (You may want to copy that last line and paste it on your computer as a reminder.) I totally understand. There will be moments where it seems like a ton of new things to learn and do. For those who feel inundated by this, please think of it as a diet or exercise program. ***All you need to do is a little bit each day.*** Don't worry about trying to accomplish everything in one or two weeks. The fact is this; it will probably take at least a month to accomplish a majority of the following tips. So just take it day by day, getting a few things done at a time. If you follow these tips I promise that your online platform, your internet presence for selling books, will benefit tremendously.

There are always tutorials that will go into great detail on any one of these tips I'm about to share. YouTube.com is an excellent place to watch videos that explain even more on how to do these things. I will touch on them all, some in more depth than others, but if you still need extra info just go to YouTube or do an internet search with "tutorial on *the subject you're looking for.*" I do this frequently, even for the research to write this book.

Ebooks versus Paper or DTB (dead tree books)

It's wise to think about having your book in print on paper *someday* but not to start. The reason is simple. You can get started with ebooks for free, and ebook sales are taking off at phenomenal rates.

"Yeah, but they can't compare with paper book sales," you might say. Don't be so sure. It's true that ebook sales were rather flat from their inception until just a few years back. Then, in November of 2007 Amazon released the Kindle, which has been followed by the Kindle 2, the Kindle DX the Kindle 3 and more versions including the Fire tablet in just four years. What's happened to ebook sales in that time? They've been soaring. And if you listen to enough Kindle owners, one thing will become clear immediately. *They love reading on that thing!* Many of them prefer it to reading actual paper books. Plus they love the convenience of carrying all of their books on one device and having the option to change fonts, sizes, browse the web, etc. (I also have a basic Kindle and a Motorola Xoom tablet, and my wife and I love them both. Plus it helps understand the customer's experience.)

And we can go beyond talking about just the Kindle. Barnes & Noble has the Nook (several models including e-ink and color tablets), Sony has the Reader, Apple's got the iPad, dozens of tablets have recently come out, and let's not ignore the cell phone. That's right. Stanza and other applications make it possible for people to read from their iPhones and other phones, so there are more and more e-reading devices popping up everywhere.

Since the Amazon Kindle has been out, ebook sales have grown exponentially. They casually went from $1.3 million in revenue for the 2nd quarter of 2002 to $8.2 million in the 4th quarter of 2007. Then Kindle and other devices emerged and sales leaped to $17 million a year later in 2008 and then skyrocketed to a whopping $56 million in the 4th quarter of 2009. While paper sales remain flat or drop, ebook sales continue to soar every year now with no end in sight.

With the iPad in the party and Barnes & Noble rolling up their sleeves while Amazon attempts to protect their turf... the battle for ebook supremacy is sure to be a fight for the ages. *Ebook sales have already surpassed paper book sales.* The shift was inevitable, but the timing took many "experts" by surprise.

Any author who is serious about her/his potential absolutely must make the book available as an ebook. Simple as that. Besides, how can one argue with the fact that it's free to do so?

Remember, the following advice is my plan for the steps to take that make the most sense, and I'll explain why as we go along. You can, however, do the following tips in any order. It's up to you, and this is why I recommend a quick read of the book entirely before getting started. And please take your time with this. It's a wealth of information that can be implemented over the coming days, weeks and even months. This is not a get-rich-quick scheme. (Don't believe people who promise instant results when selling ebooks. They are primarily luring you with false hope.)

Finally, you're going to create accounts at websites with new usernames, passwords, images, files, all kinds of things that can become a really scattered mess across your brain and computer. It'll

Social Media

Before you run off to create and upload ebooks, you'll be wise to first develop a social media network and online platform. *Your online platform can be thought of as your internet presence,* and it's **critical** for successfully marketing an ebook. The best method to begin a foundation for online platform and internet presence is by establishing a social media network in several venues. Social media is an absolute must because it not only enables you to keep in touch with friends and family, *but it also enables multiple ways to connect with absolute strangers and for absolute strangers to have multiple ways to connect with you.* Be realistic, you can't rely solely on family and friends to support you as an author. Of course you can ask for their help and for them to ask people in their circles and email lists and so on, but this will only go so far. You must reach out to strangers from all over the world and enable portals for them to connect with you.

I'm going to list several social media sites that I consider mandatory, but honestly, this category is really *the more the better.* Remember, just because you have 5 or more accounts on social media sites doesn't mean you have to be active there on a daily basis. All you need is your presence there and links to your website and ebook. Of course if you are active at some of these places it helps a lot, but it's not mandatory.

Here are several social media sites that are a must have:

Facebook.com.

This media mega-giant has over 800 million users, 50% of which log in every single day. That's amazing, 400 million users each day! The average user has 130 friends, is connected to 80 community pages-groups-events and spends nearly an hour a day on the site. 75% of users live outside the US, and Facebook is translated into 70 different languages. (Those stats are from Jan. 2012; expect the numbers to grow.) You can access it from mobile devices, and the people that do so are reportedly twice as active on the site. Needless to say, Facebook is the grand champion, number one, the big enchilada. *If you're not on Facebook, you should get on it right away. And if you are on it, you want to maximize your ability to make connections.*

So either start a Facebook account or make the most of the one you have. Upload photos and/or video of yourself. Make friends with as many people as you're comfortable doing. Comment on other people's photos and walls now and then. Manage your settings so that you get the email notifications you want. (That's all handled through your Profile page, Home tab, Account Settings under the Notifications list.) Your Privacy level can also be set through the Home tab and Privacy Settings to be made public, just for friends or custom.

You may also join multiple groups on Facebook that have to do with writing, reading, your subjects of interest, ebooks, Kindle, Nook, your genre, iPad, etc. "Groups" are designated on the FB homepage. Just click on it and search for groups. When you find ones you like, post messages on their wall as long as the *content is open for public* and tell them about your ebooks when they're ready. You can even create your own groups. Make connections and be interesting because people prefer that.

(An important note here; whenever posting anywhere, keep your messages interesting and fun without looking like a spammer. Try to add quality more than quantity. Keep posting regularly on the discussion boards, but alter them on each board so you don't get into trouble with Facebook. They have guidelines against spamming the exact same message in a cut and paste fashion to multiple boards and members.)

Now that you have your Facebook account, you'll also want a Facebook Badge, which is something you'll be able to post on your sites and other places for people to immediately click on and ask for permission from you to make a friend connection. To create a badge, just click on the Add a Badge link at the bottom of your Profile page (mine's on the left column). This will take you to your Facebook Badge page. On this page, select the Create Badge or Add a Badge option and you'll be walked through the creation process. If you already have a blog or website and know how to copy and paste the html text into a widget, you can go ahead and do that now. For those who aren't familiar with this or don't yet have a site that they can work on, we'll employ your badge later but now is a fine time to make one.

To stay organized, we're going to add our Facebook Badge html code to a Text Document and place it in our "ebooksuccess" folder. Create a new text document by placing your cursor over empty desktop space, right click, drag down to New and choose Text Document. Change the title to Facebook Badge html. Go to your Facebook Badge page, under the part that reads Choose Where to Add This Badge: click on Other. The code is in the little box below so you need to copy it by highlighting it and either using Ctrl C or right click then copy. Now you can open your Text Document for the Facebook Badge and Paste, right click and paste it into your text document. Under the File Tab choose Save As, then click on "ebooksuccess" folder for the Save In destination and then click Save. Your html code should now be properly saved in that folder to stay organized. Make a habit of doing this quick step with everything you create here, and the process will be much more organized.

You can also create a Facebook group for your ebook or a subject that interests you. Perhaps you're in the business of raising elephants and so you create a group about it. It could be Elephant Lovers or something like that, and whenever people input the search term for "elephants" they'll find you and hopefully join your group. Just click on Groups, then click Create a Group and follow the prompts.

For the purpose of this lesson, I've created a Facebook Group. It's called, How to Make, Market and Sell Ebooks - All for Free. Here's the URL; http://www.facebook.com/groups/110604178950149/. Please check it out, join our group, make a post and even pitch your story and links. There are dozens of extremely helpful people in this group, all sharing publishing experiences.

A Fan page can also be made which is similar to a Group page but subtly different. Fan pages allow users to "Like" your page with a mouse click, and they also allow certain applications such as a Storefront with Payvment where you can sell products. We'll talk more in detail about Payvment in the chapter on Other Things You Can Do, since I don't consider it a high priority location to list an ebook for sale.

To make a Fan page there's a link for Advertising at the very bottom of any Facebook page. Click on it and look for the link that says Facebook Page. Then you'll want the green button that says Create A Page. The prompts that follow will be self-explanatory and simple to do once you're already familiar with creating a profile or group page. You can use Fan pages for the name of your book or even yourself as an author though I'd recommend the book and letting your future fan-club be the ones to build a page honoring you. The implementation for the html code will be extremely similar to that of a profile badge so instead of me being redundant, just browse those instructions and that from Facebook for putting them on your website and blog when we get there.

My experience has been far better for my Group page than my Fan page, but that's because my subject matter is a How-To book which benefits from group collaboration. Some authors do better with a Fan page or just by having a normal profile. It's a personal choice, so if in doubt just begin simply with a normal profile page.

http://www.facebook.com/

Twitter.com.

Some people have amazing results with Twitter although, in my opinion, it's not as important as Facebook. Yet it's a must-have for social media. You need a Twitter account because there are exciting possibilities that exist on Twitter. You start "tweeting" regularly with things of interest and links to great articles, and people will find and follow you. It also helps to follow people who share things or deal with subjects that interest you, and these things can be "retweeted." What you'll learn on Twitter is you can write up to 140 characters and eventually connect with a lot of people. I'm not super active there, but I do have an application called Tweetdeck, which allows me to use this service even better. You can download Tweetdeck at http://www.tweetdeck.com/ or Twhirl at http://www.twhirl.org/, which basically makes using Twitter a little easier and with more options. One really nice thing about these applications is that they condense URL links to be very short in characters. If you were to write 130 characters about your ebook, plus you had a long URL link to include, Tweetdeck will automatically condense the link so that your message remains at 140 characters or less.

How does someone use Twitter to create an audience and network? Obviously you don't need to tweet about everything you're doing, like washing the dishes. Keep it interesting. Share certain anecdotes or jokes or newsworthy stuff with links as you come across them. And yes, you can tweet about your ebook and where to find it but not constantly. That would get annoying to your followers, who might be likely to "unfollow" you with a click of the mouse. "Unfollowing" is also something you can do for people who tweet more than you'd prefer.

The neat thing about Twitter is the fact that you might tweet a message others find interesting, and so they might "retweet" it and so on until it gets seen by many thousands of people. I once did a blog entry on the uses for industrial hemp, and I made a tweet about it. One person who was following me "retweeted" my mention about industrial hemp and the link to my blog site. Guess what? She had over 19,000 followers, some of whom saw my tweet and visited my blog, which received far more visitors that day than usual. The possibilities are amazing, so don't rule Twitter out. Start an account if you haven't already. You'll learn it over time.

You can also use **hash-tags** to help specify a message and gain followers faster. Hash-tags are a way of searching within the billions of tweets for topic specific posts. It's simply the number symbol or pound sign (#) with a search term, like #scifi or #kindle or even #elephant. To see if a search term is already being used, just type it in the Twitter search box at the top of the page and see how many results come up. Play around with closely related examples, like #fiction and #novel, to see which ones are more commonly used. You can even post several hash-tags in one tweet as I did about a dancing dog that went like this; Carrie the dancing dog - unreal #pets #dog #dogs #puppy #doglover #canine #animallover http://bit.ly/gs54Aj

That tweet gained me a dozen new followers immediately who also used those search terms and wouldn't have found me any other way. The same method can be used to find people with similar interests. If you follow them, there's a good chance they'll reciprocate. Ultimately, if you have a lot of readers, you may incorporate your own book title in a hash-tag. Try a Twitter search for books and authors you enjoy, like #twilight, #stevenking or #amreading. You can also play around with the terms in the Trends section, on the right of the main page.

Notice when you get a message that a new person is following you, that message will show a bit of information about them: namely how many people they follow, how many tweets they've done (which you can check and see what they have to say), and how many people are following them. Beware of people with a gross imbalance of followers to following. Say a person has zero or very few followers and is following lots of people, hundreds or thousands. That type of person is likely just building a Twitter following fast or even involved in something unscrupulous. Or if a person has many thousands of tweets, they might be such a blabber-mouth you'd rather not follow them and jam up your board with their daily ramblings, though you can also edit Notifications through your profile Settings. Remember, there's no reciprocal rule to follow someone just because they follow you. Use your best judgment and give it a go. You can always unfollow someone if needed.

Now you'll want to create a Twitter Badge. Yep, just like you did with Facebook. This badge will be a clickable link from your websites (which we'll get to for those who don't have them yet) for others to start following you. Here's a great place to get a Twitter Badge - http://www.twitterbuttons.org/. Just paste your Twitter name exactly the same in the box that asks for it, hit the Go button, and it will generate buttons to choose from. Then you copy and paste the html text code below the image you like, and when you insert it as a widget/gadget on your website or blog, it will become a cute birdie picture that people click to start following you on Twitter.

Stay organized. Follow the instructions from before to make a new text document for your Twitter Badge html code and save it in your "ebooksuccess" folder and name it "Twitter Badge html." This will be handy for grabbing when we make your blog and website.

http://www.twitter.com/

LinkedIn.

LinkedIn is the largest professional social networking site in the world. It's not just a place to put your resume, but there are other things going on at LinkedIn. With more than 135 million people from over 200 countries and territories, it's too large not to be a part of. At LinkedIn you can manage your public profile that's available for everyone to see, find and get introduced to people with connections in your specialty field. You can also be found for business opportunities, partners needed and join in discussions with likeminded individuals in private group settings. It's a smart social media site. Another bonus to being a LinkedIn member, as with Facebook, is that you'll be able to reconnect with old friends that you haven't spoken with in ages. That's a nice benefit as you're working on your online presence!

And you guessed it; LinkedIn also has badges that you can put on your sites. The process is the same. Click Edit My Profile found in the left navigation area of the home page. Click Edit Public Profile Settings in the upper right-hand corner of the Profile page. Click on the Customized Buttons link found in the Public Profile box. Choose a logo button and copy the html code provided next to it. This code will include a link to your public profile.

Stay organized and make a text document for this code and put it in your "ebooksuccess" folder. Eventually we'll paste the code into a widget of your blog and website.

http://www.linkedin.com/

Google Plus.

This may be seen as Google + or Google +1 or simply G+. It started as invitation only and became open to the public in September of 2011.

In my opinion, *Google Plus takes the best aspects of Facebook, Twitter and LinkedIn while eliminating the worst.* (However, Facebook made broad scale changes to its platform as a result of G+, so don't be surprised to see all of the venues becoming more alike in time.) Presently, Google Plus has a design that can be your one-stop for all things social media. Like Facebook, you can stream wall posts of what's happening or share comments and include video, links, photos, chat, etc. Unlike the old Facebook, you can create different "circles" that these posts go out to (though Facebook has made changes to accommodate this ability; it's just more time consuming to sort out for users who already have hundreds of FB friends). G+ circles can be composed of family, friends, work colleagues, readers, your soccer team, the bowling league, sexy lingerie club... whatever kind of circle you want to create. To me, this is a huge difference over the original Facebook as you can easily select what others do or don't see with updates and wall posts. As I said, FB made changes after Google Plus came out, but it's a hassle to change the status of friends when you have several hundred.

The G+ program will also recommend people to add and you can easily choose the circles to place them, which is a great way for them to discover you as well.

Like Twitter, anyone can add you to their circle to follow, and you can add anyone to yours. Unlike Twitter, you can identify who you want to see what, and you can do many things their platform doesn't support.

Sparks is another interesting feature that allows you to search Google Plus for content of interest. It has a list of pre-set subjects, or you can type in things like recipes, books, dog-walkers in Los Angeles or anything.

Hangout allows group video chat with multiple people, another very cool feature.

Because this social media site *does everything all the other ones do and then some,* it feels like a must for independent authors, Indies, wanting to promote their writing as well as the general population that wants the best of social media.

There are plenty of great tutorials on how to use Google Plus. Rather than trying to re-invent the wheel, let's just link some articles for you to check out if extra help is required.

http://www.readwriteweb.com/archives/how_to_start_with_google_plus.php - article tutorial

http://www.stateofsearch.com/how-to-use-google-a-quick-guide-and-thoughts-on-google-plus/ - article tutorial

http://www.youtube.com/watch?v=5TDMObxEtEY&feature
=related - video tutorial (has a brief ad but is a great video.)

You can also find badges by searching the term, *Google Plus Badges*. Here's one place I found that creates a nice photo ID for a badge - http://turhan.me/+me/. (You'll need to add the URL hyperlink of your Google Plus personal profile page when you insert it on a website or blog.)

My personal strategy is reserving Google Plus for writing-business-networking, while I use Facebook for all my friends and family, although I also use FB for my group page. Group pages for businesses, products, artists or other categories can also be made at G+ by clicking the Create button in the Manage Your Pages section under your user name.

Plus Bounce is a feature to integrate which Google Plus posts gets connected to a Facebook, Twitter and/or LinkedIn account - http://plusbounce.com/

https://plus.google.com/

Other People's Blogs (OPB).

Other people write and update blogs constantly. These blogs are on every subject under the sun and usually have comment boxes where visitors can leave replies and continue the discussion. Not only do blogs get read by many visitors for years to come, but the comments get read as well. Comment boxes often ask for a URL to go along with your message. For those who don't yet have a blog or website, we'll get to that soon. For those who do, always make sure to insert your URL address so people who read the comment can click on your link and so search engines record the connection.

It's mandatory to have something that adds to the discussion. Don't just spam messages about your book but add something helpful to the conversation or topic. Showing you can assist, add value or entertain others will do much more to get people to click on your link. You can also type out the full URL address within the comment, which typically will become a clickable link.

Note that comments often require approval from the blog owner before they get published. But as long as it's something useful *blog owners usually approve comments because they want it to appear that many people read their blog*. Once your comment is posted it will act like a billboard for you and your site for years to come. One smart blog comment and link can literally attract hundreds of visitors or more to your site over time. Imagine what you can do by leaving comments on a few blogs every single day. Over the years that can add up to incredibly valuable free marketing. It's not an exaggeration to say many thousands of clicks per year are attainable by simply making three smart blog comments per day.

So how do you find all these blogs where you'd like to leave comments?

Google Alerts.

This is not a social media site but a social media tool. Google Alerts are incredibly helpful for anyone marketing online. I use them for my book titles, for my name and also for subjects of interest like self-publishing and ebooks. For those who aren't familiar with Google Alerts, this is how the company describes them; *Google Alerts are email updates of the latest relevant Google results (web, news, etc.) based on your choice of query or topic. Some handy uses of Google Alerts include:*

-monitoring a developing news story
-keeping current on a competitor or industry
-getting the latest on a celebrity or event
-keeping tabs on your favorite sports teams

But I use them to help me with marketing efforts and finding blogs of similar subject matter. For example, I get alerts each day about anything on the subject of making and selling ebooks. I can then click on those links and read the current articles and blogs. Usually there will be a comment box where I can leave a helpful comment and include a small blurb about my ebook and a link. As long as I'm not blatantly spamming an advertisement, it's really easy to get my message and links out there for others to click on. This helps generate traffic and rise in search engine rankings over time. Sometimes ten or more people will click on my link that same day from reading just one blog comment.

To get started, visit the site - http://www.google.com/alerts and fill out the form with your search terms and a return email. Once a day or so, Google will email you with any web content that appears. Then visit those articles and blog posts. If there's a comment box, leave a thoughtful reply and insert your URL which will be a clickable part of your name next to your comment. You can often type in a URL in the box itself that will become clickable. I recommend leaving at least two or three comments per day so your potential for new visitors will increase dramatically over the following weeks and months.

Remember, comments often require the moderator to approve them, but blog hosts usually do because it shows that people read their blog. No bloggers enjoy seeing their comment boxes reading zero, even me.

Amazon.com.

That's right; I said Amazon and social media in the same category. The reason is because *Amazon has a huge forum* in the Kindle Books section. To participate you have to be a customer of Amazon, which means you must have bought something, no matter how cheap, at some point in time. Then you can create a profile with your photo, description and link to your site (we'll get there). Once your profile is in place you can go to the Kindle Books Department or Kindle Store and hit the tab for Discussions. Here's the link - http://www.amazon.com/tag/kindle/forum/. There's also specific discussions through the Community Directory, then click the Literature, Arts & Sciences tab, then you can specify your genre like Adventure, Romance or even random topics like Post-Apocalyptic. You can also input search terms and find exactly what you're looking for. There's the general, main forum under the Discussions tab where by far the most people visit. Throughout these forums you'll find thousands of people posting all sorts of topics ranging from how much they love reading on their Kindle to new ebooks to the politics of the publishing industry and more. There are courtesies to follow and specific posts for new authors to introduce themselves, *but beware of spamming these people.* It's against the rules, and they won't take kindly to posts about you and your ebook. Specific sections and threads exist for Indie authors to introduce themselves and that's the best place to start. Follow forum etiquette and only make posts relevant to the thread topics. Be interesting and helpful wherever possible, and then you can add links to your book. If you get along with these people, you'll be surprised how many of them will buy your ebooks, especially if they're priced reasonably to start.

In May of 2011, a ***Meet Our Authors*** forum was designated especially for Independent authors at http://www.amazon.com/forum/meet%20our%20authors where they can do much more self-promotion without violating the TOS (terms of service).

For UK residents, notice for most any book or product which exists at both Amazon in the US and the UK, all it takes to make the transition is changing the suffix ".com" to ".co.uk" as in http://www.amazon.com/Make-Market-Sell-Ebooks-ebook/dp/B003CJU49I/ for the US version of this book to the UK version, http://www.amazon.co.uk/Make-Market-Sell-Ebooks-ebook/dp/B003CJU49I/. Others countries with their own Amazon store simply change the .com to a different suffix, like Amazon.de for Germany, Amazon.fr for France, .es for Spain, .it for Italy, .co.jp for Japan, etc. It Germany, this book is http://www.amazon.de/Make-Market-Sell-Ebooks-ebook/dp/B003CJU49I/.

http://www.amazon.com

In a similar thread, here are some other places for readers and authors to get together:

Kindleboards, for Kindle readers and Indie authors - http://www.kindleboards.com/

NookBoards, for Nook owners and Indie authors - http://www.nookboards.com/forum/

Goodreads, for readers and authors in general - http://www.goodreads.com/

Shelfari, Amazon's online book club - http://www.shelfari.com/

Forums in General.

Whatever your subject is about, it's a pretty sure bet there are forums dedicated to that somewhere. Find these forums and participate. For example, a simple Google search for "elephant forums" or "elephant lovers" should result in places to meet and great likeminded people.

You can also create forums within your website once we get there. Some sites for Indie authors and readers:

http://indiespot.myfreeforum.org/ - a place for readers and authors to connect.

http://redroom.com/ - where the writers are.

http://www.authonomy.com/ - where writers become authors and more.

http://www.inkpop.com/ - for YA (Young Adult) authors and readers.

There are hundreds of other social media sites and tools. Because this field is growing exponentially, I'm only going to discuss and touch on a few of them.

MySpace.com.

MySpace is primarily for kids and younger adults, so if you're a young writer or have subject matter suited for this audience, then

MySpace is also a site to consider. There are reading groups aplenty on MySpace, not as many as Facebook but still a sizeable potential market. At MySpace, you can create as simple or complex a page as you want, make friends and get noticed. You can post samples of your writing, photos, videos and more to let people know you and your stories. Surprisingly, MySpace has just recently introduced its own badges. So this is an opportunity to demonstrate how to make one from scratch. Simply copy and save a MySpace logo image (found easily in a Google Image search), upload it to your site and then insert a link to your MySpace page. And yes, we will cover this in more detail in the blog section, but for now just copy a MySpace logo image and save it in your "ebooksuccess" folder.

http://www.myspace.com/

YouTube.com.

You might not think of this at first as a place to promote your writing but it can certainly be done, especially if you're fairly handy with video. A simple video on you and your book can easily be seen by hundreds and even thousands of people in little time. Watch some YouTube videos on books to get a feel for what others are doing and decide if those ideas might work for you. Some authors read sample chapters. Others talk about the themes within the book. And some come up with imagery from photos and video to give the viewer an idea of what the book is about. For my YouTube videos, I give examples of free advice and include my websites for those who are interested in learning more. Here's an example of a basic video I made (when my book first came out with an older cover) that's led to dozens of sales - http://www.youtube.com/watch?v=ZTbCeFXM9y4.

The nice thing about these videos is the amount of possible views they can get and the fact that some people relate better to video than to printed ads. As my example shows, you don't have to produce Oscar quality movies. As long as a video speaks to the viewer, they may likely buy your book.

Even if you're not making a video, YouTube is also a place to leave comments similar to blog comments although they tend to get bumped down the list quickly over time (depending on how popular the video is). You can't leave complete URL links as for blogs, but you can mention your book and cleverly leave a URL as just the domain name. Again, make sure to leave helpful or entertaining comments and not come across like a spammer.

Definitely consider possibilities with YouTube in terms of blurbs about your book in ways that might gather some traffic to your sites. There are also badges for YouTube or you can create links to your profile page. You can also embed YouTube videos into your blog and website when we get there.

http://www.youtube.com

Yahoo Answers.

Yahoo has an enormous forum under the title of Yahoo Answers. Both questions and answers exist from people all over the world for every subject imaginable. There's a section in particular for Books and Authors, and there are also plenty of sections for topics that might be related to your ebook like environment, pets, health, sports, travel and more.

You can browse the most recent questions or search for questions pertaining to your ebook subject. Then it's good to answer the question in a helpful manner. You can also leave a URL link within the answer box or the resource box. The good thing about Yahoo Answers is that they act as blog posts where people researching questions for months and years later can still stumble upon your answer, especially if it's chosen as the best answer and placed in the top of the results. Be sure to look for recent questions that are unresolved by tailoring your search to be for Open Questions (status) or posts submitted within the last seven days.

http://answers.yahoo.com/

Others to consider:
http://www.flickr.com/ - for sharing images.

http://www.digg.com/ - general social site and place where you can recommend blogs and sites. (Like for your own once we get there.)

http://www.metacafe.com/ - videos.

http://www.stumbleupon.com/ - discover cool stuff.

http://www.technorati.com/ - a collection of blogs and a great place to search for blogs of interest. It's also a fantastic place to submit articles provided you have been accepted to write for them.

http://www.delicious.com/ - general social site.

http://www.klout.com/ - a place to connect all your links and measure online influence.

Remember, there are literally hundreds of others. One could write several books on this topic alone, so please understand if I haven't mentioned a social media site you enjoy. Even if you just do a portion of what I've recommended, these venues will be of tremendous value as you create links to your blog and websites as well as when you upload ebooks to retailers. You don't have to be super-active or try to do them all, nor would I recommend it, but make sure you are in at least three of these and use Google Alerts. Facebook, Google Plus and Twitter are the most important to me, but this is a personal choice.

Deciding on a Domain Name

Before you run off and create any website or blog, take some quality time (as in hours or even days) to think about and research the domain name you'd like. It might be catchy while conveying some aspects of you, your book or business. It will also help dramatically with search engines if the words within the URL domain name are related to any possible internet search terms for someone looking for what you have to offer. As an example, let's say your book teaches others how to build solar birdbaths and you also sell them as well. Your website could be named solarbirdbath.com. That would help a bunch if someone wanted a solar powered birdbath with a fountain and heated water, and so they went searching online by typing the phrase "solar birdbath." Hard to believe, but it's actually a term which gets typed into Google searches 8,100 times per month (Jan. 2012). As for the plural of the phrase, "solar birdbaths," that only gets searched 2,900 times a month in comparison or about 28% as much. Based on this data, it would be smarter to name your site solarbirdbath.com than solarbirdbaths.com. Surprisingly, the "s" at the end makes a difference with search engines, which attempt to give searchers exactly what they're seeking.

So homework is mandatory to discover which terms and phrases related to your website title will be searched the most and how much competition from other advertisers exists already. How did I come up with those statistics and how will you do similar research?

By using Google Keyword Tool External and researching keywords in general. This advice is not just for making websites but for research before everything you post online about your book (Amazon description, blog titles and text body, articles, press releases, etc).

It's my belief that *keywords are essential* to help search engines like Google, Yahoo and Bing link any webpage to certain words, terms or phrases. There are literally hundreds of search engines the world over, but you only need to focus on the big three. (Actually, if you only focused on Google, you'd be okay here, or if you live in Asia—focus on Baidu.) It's best to add keywords to every site, blog and location that has boxes for them: keywords that describe the content of what your site and book are about. And, as shown above, you can even figure out ways to include keywords in your domain name.

For example, let me explain how I came to decide on the title for another book and the websites for it. The book is entirely focused on teaching others to create free websites and blogs. During the initial brainstorming sessions, I wrote down the major keywords and phrases that came to mind. Here's the partial list:

Create free website
Build free website
Make free website
Make free site
How to build free sites
Create free blog
Make a free blog
How to make free websites
Make my own website
Make your own website
My free blog

Your free website

And so on and so on. The very next step is to go to Google Keyword Tool External https://adwords.google.com/select/KeywordToolExternal. There you can input these phrases individually or altogether and get valuable feedback from Google on which search terms are used the most and how much competition exists from other advertisers. By comparing each of these plus the synonyms, or similar terms Google automatically provides, it becomes clear which keywords should work best over time.

Back to our example. By comparing extremely similar phrases like "create free website," to "build free website" and "make free website," Google told me that "make free website" was a more common search term than the others. I also learned that "website" is more commonly searched than "site" and "blog" when mixed with the rest of the phrase. Another revelation was that "your" was more commonly searched than "my" when mixed with these other phrases. I also wanted to include the word "own" because it implies ownership and only slightly reduced the number of searches per month. Turns out "your free website" gets searched 165,000 times per month while "your own free website" gets 90,500 searches (Jan. 2012). Even though it's a lot, that's actually a difference I can live with for a word that helps the title have more power for the consumer. Making sense?

In less than an hour I had narrowed my book title and website URL down to these possibilities:

Make your own free website
How to make your own free website
Your own free website

I checked the competition from other advertisers which is also included in the Keyword Tool results. It turns out when comparing "make your own free website" to "your own free website," the searches per month were identical with Google with similar competition from other advertisers. (The advent of Google Panda seems to have affected these results, but that's more SEO than we're going to get into now.)

Then I checked name availability at both GoDaddy and the websites where I wanted to create free examples for that book. Although the domain name was not available at GoDaddy as a pure dot com, it was available at the venues to create my examples. And so I went ahead and registered it as yourownfreewebsite.webs.com and yourownfreewebsite.yolasite.com. (Know this; it doesn't matter if you have a long domain name. People click links to visit sites so your domain can be long. If that still bugs you or you feel it looks unprofessional, a change to a pure dot com is only about $10 per year.)

Additionally I battled with whether to use dashes, underscores or nothing to separate the words in the URL. Should the site be called your-own-free-website, or your_own_free_website or simply yourownfreewebsite? All of the research indicated that Google would find my site just fine in any case since they have such a complex algorithm with over 200 variables for detecting keywords, so this really boils down to personal preference. In the end I liked it this way, your-own-free-website.com because I believe it's the easiest way to read. Remember, you don't have to use dashes or underscores for Google to find the keywords in a URL. For that site I did spend a few bucks to have the custom domain name without the extra suffix, though for demonstration purposes I also created your-own-free-website.webs.com to show others not to worry about the extra suffix.

Finally, I wanted to name the book, *How to Make Your Own Free Website*. I went to Amazon and typed that exact phrase into a book search and was delighted to see that no one had a book with that title. Surprisingly, there were very few titles even close to that, so I knew this would be a great name for people to find not only my website but my Amazon book as well. I included the subtitle for those who wanted more info on blogs and the title became, *How to Make Your Own Free Website: And Your Free Blog Too.* This way the keywords are part of the URL address and the book title, and **over time** people will certainly find me with search engine terms.

(Side note; even if someone already has a book with the same title that you'd like use, that doesn't copyright the title. There can be many books with the same title, like *The Big Bang.* You just can't have a book named *Harry Potter and The Big Bang* because the character, Harry Potter, is copyrighted material.)

So take your time not only brainstorming for names but also using Google Keyword Tool External to research the intelligence of your options. ***Ideally you can find some keywords that have low competition from other advertisers and high numbers of searches from users each month.***

This advice is also wise for anything you post online, whether a blog post, article, etc. This tool will help you quickly choose the very best keywords along the way.

https://adwords.google.com/select/KeywordToolExternal

Remember to also check a URL name availability as purely a .com as in solarbirdbath.com, because someday you may want to spend a few bucks and make the conversion. Name availability is easy to check at many places including GoDaddy - http://www.godaddy.com/. If you find the perfect name for your website, such as solarbirdbath.com, and a registrar like GoDaddy confirms that it is available, then you might want to spend up to $10 per year to reserve that domain name even if you're not ready to install it. The reason is so it will be there when it's needed, and no one can take it from you. Even if the dot com is not available, there are also options like solarbirdbath.info, solarbirdbath.net, solarbirdbath.biz and solarbirdbath.me.

Next step, let's look at blogging hosts with site-building software.

Creating Your Blog Site

Okay, we're finally here after I kept mentioning we'd get here. Whew!

What's the difference between a blog and a website? Great question. Actually there's not a whole lot of difference at some level. I like to think of my blog as my dynamic, ever-changing, up to the minute site while my website is more of a set piece that only changes occasionally. Characteristics that set most blogs apart from websites are: entries are a series of posts, they're arranged by date of entry, they usually have comment boxes for visitors, often an RSS feed (Really Simple Syndication) or subscription link, previous posts are categorized by month and archived, and they often don't have an email account associated with them.

Blogs don't have to be updated regularly; they're just designed to do so easily. They can have totally static pages and can function very much like a website. Both blogs and websites are extremely important, and both can be acquired and easily designed for free. If you only have the time or energy to get one up and running, however, make it a blog (for the dynamic aspects) and we'll build your webpages later.

A lot of people have no idea how important a blog site can be to their online platform. You can think of your blog as your home base, the one area that leads to everything else online about you. At the blog site you can have as much information about you as you want, plus it can be updated regularly to provide links to all the other websites that offer your ebook for sale (which we'll get to soon). Your blog site is absolutely essential if you want to maximize your success with this. Fortunately, there are free places to create a blog. Notice, for the free domain name your site will have a URL like yourdomainname.wordpress.com or yourdomainname.blogger.com, but it really doesn't matter. The vast majority of people click links to get to websites; they don't have to manually type or remember a URL's name. (Except in examples like this book where some of the readers will have to retype the links. I know I just contradicted myself, but it's true. Your domain name can be really long these days because most people will visit it with a click of the mouse.)

Also note that some websites have blog capabilities like an "add on" to the website. I prefer blogging hosts that are solely designed for blogging since I believe they function better, though this is a personal preference. Here are some options for free blog sites:

Wordpress.com.

(Note that Wordpress.com is a free blog while Wordpress.org is paid hosting.)

Wordpress is a favorite, and one of the biggies I recommend. It's consistently mentioned in the best free blog sites and usually it's listed as number one. It's an easy to use, hosted blog service that allows you to create an unlimited number of blogs (and pages) and submits your site to the Google blog directory. Wordpress is also noted for its excellent traffic-monitoring stats and search engine rankings. Another nice thing about the free version of Wordpress is that they don't load your blog with paid advertising, which some other free blog sites do, although they will add an ad in rare moments to help pay costs. You can use their page templates or customize one to fit your needs as well as load one totally from scratch. Plus they give you a whopping 3GB (3,000MB) of storage space, which is a ton compared to any other free service. What more could you want, right? With Wordpress, you can follow their tutorials for any question to make a professional looking blog site in very little time. They also have an excellent support forum. I highly recommend giving Wordpress a try if you haven't yet.

(Side note; before you create your blog, take a few minutes, hours or even days to think about the domain name you'd like. It might be catchy while conveying some aspects of you or your ebook. It will also help with search engines if words within the domain name are related to any possible internet search terms (e.g., elephantlovers.wordpress.com). You'll also want to check its availability as purely a .com as in elephantlovers.com, because someday you may want to spend a few bucks and make the conversion. Name availability is easy to check at many places including GoDaddy - http://www.godaddy.com/.)

Back to Wordpress. For the purpose of this instruction and ebook, I've used Wordpress.com to create a totally free blog site as an example. You can find it here at http://ebooksuccess4free.wordpress.com. Initially, it took me just a few hours to create three relatively attractive web pages. (Don't feel bad if it takes you longer, as I'm more experienced at this than some.) I regularly update the home page while many of the other pages remain somewhat static aside from visitor comments.

Now, when you visit my site you can scroll down and see on the sidebar where I've added my badges! The Facebook, Twitter, Google Plus and LinkedIn badges are all there. Aha, now it makes sense that the social media is in place, so when the blog is created those links can easily be inserted. As a follow-up with action call, I encourage you to click on them and make a connection with me. Where applicable, please include the words "ebook success" or a personal note in your message so I'll know where you came from (otherwise it might appear as spam). I'll be happy to make friends and follow you in your endeavors. I also hope you'll leave a comment somewhere on my blog page with the link to your site for myself and others to click on.

If you're just starting out with Wordpress.com for a blog, here are some basics to get you going. After you sign up, you'll need to Register a blog. There you enter a blog name of your choice and a blog title that should be like a headline. Click to enter and Login. You should be sent to a Dashboard for your page, like a command central. Near the middle of the Dashboard page is a button that says Change Theme. Click on that and browse hundreds of choices from Random, A to Z, to Popular themes. And you can always change the template later without losing your work. After choosing a template, get started creating a blog, even a throw-away entry that you'll toss later just to get a feel for the process. As you blog along, click Update or Visit Site to save changes and check its appearance. From the editing area, it's always a good idea to place your cursor over the little icons for an explanation of what they do. You'll quickly become familiar with them and the whole process. For instance, when you're typing a blog post, if the area feels too small to work in there's an icon like a computer screen that says Toggle Fullscreen Mode and gives you a larger work space.

It would take an entire book to completely tutor someone to use Wordpress, but fortunately there's an excellent support forum with thorough answers to almost any question. If not, you can always ask a question and get tailored advice. Also do a Wordpress tutorial search on YouTube, and you'll have dozens of instructional videos to choose from.

If you use Wordpress.com, here's the way to insert your badge widgets. Once you've created your home page, open the tab My Dashboard. Scroll down on the left and look for Appearance. Under that is a tab for Widgets. Click on that and a host of Widget options appear that you can click/drag from the center to the upper right of the page to employ them into your Sidebar. The widget called Text for Arbitrary Text or HTML is the one that you want to drag to your upper right corner to employ as a Badge on your page. When you've done that you can open the box for editing by clicking the down arrow. Let's use Facebook for an example. Open the Text box with the down arrow, and type in "Facebook" (or whatever you choose) into the Title area. Underneath that is where you'll paste the html text code that you get from your Facebook Badge. You may have to backtrack to get that done unless you saved it in your "ebooksuccess" folder. (If you have to backtrack to another website, remember to open multiple windows when doing this so you don't leave and lose the page you're working with.) Once you've retrieved and copied the Facebook Badge's html text, go back to the Wordpress Text widget and paste it in there. Click the Save button. Then go above and click the Visit Site button and **presto,** you should see your Facebook Badge on your blog. Click on it to check that it works. Then do this process for Twitter, LinkedIn and any other social media badge you have. All of these widgets can be moved around by dragging from the widget page. Cool, huh? I get a real kick when I see these things in place, so hopefully you will too.

How do you create your own badge for something like MySpace or anything else you want to link to? There are a few ways, but the main thing is to create a URL of the image. One way is to Add a New Post on Wordpress and insert a picture by clicking next to the Upload/Insert tab the icon that says Add an Image. It will prompt you to Select Files, where you will probably get it from your computer's Desktop, My Documents, My Pictures or in that "ebooksuccess" folder if you're really organized. Once you select the image it will upload and then ask where you want it and how big you want it. You can choose any size, but I prefer medium to smaller images. (Sizes can be altered later.) Once you click Insert into Post, your desired image will be there. You can View your site, click on the image and notice that it creates an entire page with a URL address for that image alone. Copy that URL address, go back to your Dashboard, Appearances, Widgets, and drag an Image Widget to the right side and insert it. You can name it as you like, but be sure to paste the URL address of your image into the Image URL box, and then copy and paste the destination page (the URL of your MySpace profile page for this example) into the Link URL (when the image is clicked) box. You can also easily adjust the Width and Height in pixels here to any size you want. Click Save, Visit Site and *voila,* your newly created widget is in place and functioning properly. You may have to adjust the size through the widget control and play around with pixel width and height. (Notice I have created a Goodle Plus badge this way as an example at http://www.ebooksuccess4free.wordpress.com. It's just an Image widget with a link to my Google Plus profile page.)

There's another way to create URLs of images and documents (which will come in handy when we load sample chapters later to your sites). This way is through a site called - http://www.docstoc.com/. It works very much like what we just went through, so instead of explaining it all again just visit their site and they'll walk you through a similar process. (I'll also cover Docstop in more detail when we upload sample chapters, so let's wait until then.)

Also when you create a blog with Wordpress, you want to verify it with the big 3 search engines here - http://en.support.wordpress.com/webmaster-tools/. This link is for verifying your site with Google, Yahoo and Bing search engines (which we'll cover again in the SEO chapter). It will assist you to add metatags to your site that these search engines will eventually crawl and identify. Help with this can also be found through the Dashboard of your blog. If you scroll down the left side you'll find a tab that says Tools. Click on it and scroll down to the Webmaster Verification Tools. There you will see the boxes that go hand in hand with the metatags you'll be asked to input by using the link above to visit the big 3 search engines. And this will help too - http://en.support.wordpress.com/search-engines/ as a tutorial for the process and answers to frequent questions.

Wordpress has very few cons, primarily that they don't allow JavaScript (can be dangerous and used maliciously). Because they don't allow certain types of coding, it means some applications, like PayPal buttons, are a bit trickier to implement. (I'll give a detailed tutorial on implementing PayPal buttons to Wordpress blogs later. For now, just get familiar with creating pages, making posts, uploading images and inserting links.)

So please check out Wordpress, and if it looks good just take your time and work on creating your blog when you can. Before you know it, you'll be blogging like a champ. (Note; your home page is designed to be changed and updated regularly, while other pages you create are designed to be more static. You can update the other pages, just in editing style and without creating a new comment box.)

Below is the tutorial page for uploading documents while the next one is a list of supported formats for images, documents, audio and video.

http://en.support.wordpress.com/uploading-documents/

I did an example blog for newbies to upload sample chapters at this link where they can see the process - http://ebooksuccess4free.wordpress.com/2010/03/07/inserting-sample-chapter-links-for-newbies-on-wordpress/.

http://en.support.wordpress.com/accepted-filetypes/ - a list of supported file types.

http://www.wordpress.com/

Blogger.com.

Blogger is the other biggie I like. It has been around since 1999 and was bought by Google in 2002. It's extremely popular, user-friendly, ad-free, and since Blogger's owned by Google it's also perfect for signing up with AdSense, Google Affiliate Network and being listing in the Google directory. (Blogger calls widgets "Gadgets," and they work the same as on Wordpress.) Blogger also doesn't have premade PayPal buttons, but it's very easy to create and add a PayPal button as an HTML/Javascript Gadget, which we'll explain in detail in the Selling from Your Websites chapter. Blogger has tons of customizable template choices plus a great tutorial area and forum. Blogger is where I started my first blog, http://www.thebigbangauthor.com (costs $10/year to have the custom domain name), and I've been extremely happy with it. Since using Wordpress, I wouldn't choose Blogger over Wordpress, but it's a fine place to create a blog. People constantly argue over which is better. I prefer Blogger for ease of use, but my Wordpress site does better with SEO results and traffic. Wordpress also currently has more detailed stat monitoring.

Gadget badges work here basically the same as they do on Wordpress. The process of getting there is as follows; after signing in you'll need to click on the Customize or Layout tab. It will direct you to a page where you can view your Navbar, Header, Gadgets (widgets) and Footer. Clicking on Add a Gadget will give you the options to choose from. For badges, you'll want to click on HTML/Java Script and then follow the previous tutorial to copy and paste the html text code. Once you've Saved it, you can View your site and *abracadabra,* your badge should be in place. As with Wordpress, there are tons of other gadgets/widgets you can play around with and decide what you like best. This is a great habit to get into; play around with these things to see what works well and what doesn't. You can always make changes later plus you might find some pleasant discoveries.

As in Wordpress, when you're making a new post you can view and work with it in Edit Html mode (which is more tech savvy) or you can choose the Compose mode which is WYSIWYG (what you see is what you get). The Preview button will give a quick glimpse of what your post will look like. Again, make a post just to get a feel for the process since you can always edit or delete it later.

Unfortunately, adding sample chapters (like the pdf file we did above) on Blogger is a bit more complex. Since there's no way to directly upload a pdf file into Blogger, I needed to embed one by creating either an embedded HTML or a URL page of the pdf file. I went to - http://www.docstoc.com/ and signed up for the free account. Then I was able to upload my sample chapter pdf file there, follow their prompts and eventually insert it into my blog post. (We'll talk about different formats in the Formatting chapter.)

The embedded version also works well, just a bit trickier. I had to make the width dimensions smaller so it would fit in the page, though any reader can click on the Full Screen option if they want to read it without a magnifying glass. Actually, it works fine.

If you'd like to see exactly what I'm talking about, here's the blog on the sample chapter I inserted with this method - http://www.thebigbangauthor.com/2010/03/inserting-links-for-newbies.html.

https://www.blogger.com/start

For most of you, Wordpress or Blogger would be fine. I'm recommending Wordpress overall, but the one thing I like more about Blogger is that they allow Javascript gadgets. A good idea is to Google the phrase, "Wordpress vs. Blogger" to get other viewpoints. Common opinions are that Wordpress is more professional though Blogger is easier to use. Actually, you'll find a range of pros and cons for each. A biggie for some bloggers; they don't like the fact that Google owns Blogger and can shut down your blog if they find your content objectionable while Wordpress is Open Source so blogs can be about anything and not get shut down. I must report having far better search engine results with Wordpress, which is odd since Blogger is owned by Google. However, I'm keeping both. Ultimately, this is a personal decision so please take time to research this. Or you can do what I do and make a blog on each host. Why not? It's free and you can link them to each other.

Livejournal.com.

Livejournal is another free blogging service. I haven't used it personally, but it ranks fairly high with ease of use and design tools, yet it falls short in stat monitoring and technical assistance. It's mostly preferred by site owners who enjoy adding their own CSS (Cascading Style Sheets).

http://www.livejournal.com/

As with everything on these lists, there are more options if you merely use search engines to find them. I'm just pointing out the most popular and likely the best for your needs. Here are a few more:

http://www.blogabond.com/ - dedicated to traveling and maps.

http://www.blog.com/ - offers unlimited bandwidth for free.

http://www.blogster.com/ - catered for photos and video, also offers free image hosting.

http://www.tblog.com/ - focus on generating community based traffic.

Finally on blogging, remember to add keywords, labels, categories and/or tags wherever boxes present themselves to do so. (We'll discuss this is greater detail in the SEO chapter.) These are general terms that describe the subjects of your post to help search engines and people find your blog. You can also add your name to these boxes as that will help with branding. Advice on blogging would generate an entire book itself, so please look for experts in the field who dedicate their blogs teaching others how to blog more effectively. A Google search will lead you to outfits like this one - http://www.contentrobot.com/, and there are many more. These people have written volumes on blogging and have excellent advice to make the most of any effort.

Next step; every book needs a cover and you might as well create one for free.

Cover Design

Okay, we're switching gears from building your online platform to creating your ebooks. We'll be talking about cover design, formatting and uploading to retail venues. As a heads up for some readers who may already have a lovely cover design and don't want to get overwhelmed by formatting but would rather move straight to uploading via Amazon, Smashwords and others; feel free to skip these chapters for now and come back to formatting (for your own sites) after you've done the uploading venues. For the rest of you, let's move into cover design.

Of course we all know that covers are important; *people do judge books by their cov*ers. And while you might be tempted to abandon ship and spend anywhere from $50 to a few hundred to over a thousand dollars enlisting professional help, which is not a bad idea either, I'll argue that an effective cover can be designed absolutely for free. Another thing you really should do is check out the top selling books on Amazon - http://www.amazon.com/gp/bestsellers/books/. These are paper books, not ebooks, and it may surprise you to see how plain, simple and in some cases, unattractive, many of the covers are. It should not only surprise you, but it should inspire you knowing that books with average covers can still sell, and that you can come up with something at least as good if not better. The ultimate success of a book is determined by what's inside, and the fact that many of these best-sellers have less than amazing covers is evidence of that. Another benefit to browsing multiple book covers is that it may help generate ideas on what will work for yours. (Actually, cheap help can be found at Smashwords for both cover design and formatting by sending an email asking for these things to list@smashwords.com. But I prefer to do it myself, especially because I have multiple books and often like making small changes.)

Remember, ebook covers are normally seen as fairly small pictures. That means people don't inspect them up close and detect minor flaws that may annoy them if they were browsing in a bookstore. *Tiny flaws won't affect purchasers as they browse your cover on their computer screen.* For simple yet effective designs, there are many things you can do for free; all of which can provide quality images and text for your covers. I'm going to list several methods for obtaining and working with images at home and online.

Take photos yourself.

Use a digital camera and take photos either of yourself or things that are in line with the themes in your book. Many cover images include the author or background landscapes that are simple pictures with appropriate text around them. With image/graphic editing software (we'll cover below) you can handle additions that will complement your photo. Or you can take photos of something related to your ebook. I did this for my first novel, *The Little Universe.* I asked a friend who is an artist to hold out her arm with a paintbrush in hand. She stood in front of a black background, and the resulting photo worked great. The parts I wanted to keep were her arm and paintbrush, and they were cut out with a free editing program and pasted over another image, a public domain one.

Public domain images.

Public domain means anything that is not owned by someone with copyright restrictions. Like Open Source, it's free for everyone to use so long as they're not selling it. For a book cover, public domain pictures are fair game. I also used a public domain image for *The Little Universe*. It's a photo of an actual spiral galaxy taken by the Hubble Space telescope. Since NASA is a government outfit paid for by our tax dollars, the American people collectively own those images. If you like amazing astronomy pictures then definitely see the collection at http://www.hubblesite.org/gallery/. However, most of your ebooks probably won't have much to do with astronomy, so I've got places for the rest of you. Here's a list of websites that offer literally tens of thousands of free, public domain images you can use:

http://www.photos8.com/

http://www.public-domain-photos.com/

http://www.publicdomainpictures.net/

http://www.public-domain-image.com/

http://www.pdphoto.org/

http://www.usa.gov/Topics/Graphics.shtml

http://www.flickr.com/creativecommons/ - free with permission (more on this below).

Isn't it amazing how many images are out there that you can use absolutely for free? Again, this is a partial list while an internet search will find other sites.

(Side note; if you want to cheat just a little, you can buy royalty free images for about a couple of bucks apiece. I did this for my second novel, *Jim's Life*. I paid two dollars for the rights to use an image of a young man's hands with colorful light energy all around them. It was perfectly in line with the theme of my novel, and I was delighted that something like that existed. I found that image by searching Google for royalty free images. There are dozens of places where you can browse millions of images and pictures for book covers and buy them for about one to four dollars apiece. You can also search the stock photos by keywords to narrow the results.)

There are plenty, but here are two great sites for royalty free images:

http://www.bigstockphoto.com/ - where I got the image for *Jim's Life*.

http://www.istockphoto.com/ - another place I like and very affordable.

Photo and Image Editing software.

These products are much easier to use and less to install than graphic software. Photo editing might be all you need for creating a simple yet pleasing book cover. I used Picasa 3 to easily manipulate the images and add some text to my novels although Picasa is severely limited in what it can do compared to graphic editors. But even if you end up getting more complex software, I recommend Picasa or Flickr if you don't already have either. People argue over which one is better, but for the purposes of creating an ebook cover, Picasa is great. It's free, managed by Google and it's super user-friendly. Simply download Picasa 3 and follow the prompts. When you want to add photos or images, open Picasa and click the Import button. It will ask from what source and you'll most likely choose the Folder option where you can then check the origin and individual photos or entire folders to upload. Check the little Upload box, choose your Share options and click Import All. Then you can start editing your images just by clicking them to open. Picasa has tutorials for more information as does YouTube. When you're happy with what you've done, under the File tab choose Export Picture to Folder, then Browse your Desktop for the "ebooksuccess" folder, click to highlight it and hit OK and then Export. Your edited picture will now be either in the open or in the "ebooksuccess" folder.

(As a side note here; whenever you upload any images to Facebook, your blog site, etc, it's best to use a photo imaging tool like Picasa or Flickr to correct minor imperfections beforehand. Fixing things like red-eye, poor back light, fuzzy focus and cropping are simple fixes that often involve one click and will make your uploads look much better. Flickr doesn't have editing software, but it has a free partner in Picnik that does. If you use Picasa's one button for fixing most everything, the I'm Feeling Lucky button, it might become one of your good friends. Cropping is almost always a good idea too.)

There is a very special aspect to Flickr that I love. They have a category called Creative Commons, which is a huge inventory of photos that can be freely used as long as the artist is credited or gives permission. To check this out visit Flickr, use the search box for the subject matter, then click on Advanced Search. Scroll down for the Creative Commons box and check that to display results that are free to use. Then check with the artist for permission. I used two Flickr photos this way for a short story I posted on Amazon - http://www.amazon.com/Extreme-Skiing-Psychedelic-Mushrooms-ebook/dp/B005OZJ1JC/.

Here's the short list of photo/image editing software, and more are available through a search:

http://www.picasa.google.com/ - perfect for simple things like image enhancement, cropping, resizing and text additions.

http://www.flickr.com/ - similar to Picasa, owned by Yahoo, preferred by people who want to share their photos with potentially large communities and by many avid Wordpress bloggers.

Open Source Image and Graphic Editors.

These are more complicated and capable than Picasa, but if you're familiar with the original Macintosh Paint program or Microsoft Paint, then it's not that far of a stretch to learn how to use these types of software. These programs can alter your images in every way imaginable, and they can also create outstanding images entirely from scratch. Remember to watch tutorials, and I also recommend following along with video lessons and attempting to do the same things in real time. (Some instructors are better than others. I can vouch for tutor4u who teaches Inkscape on YouTube in that he's easy to follow.)

Using one of these graphic editors is how I made the cover of this ebook, *How to Make, Market and Sell Ebooks - All for Free.* I used Inkscape and was a total beginner. The cover design probably won't win any awards, but it's arguably as good as some of the best-selling books I've found on Amazon. And that's good enough for me. Remember, books are ultimately judged by the value within, and people mostly read books that are recommended to them. Would you rather have a lack-luster cover for a book with 5-star reviews and plenty of referrals or a fantastic cover on a book full of 1-star reviews that warn others to stay away? I'll take the first option.

Here's the partial list of sites with free editing software:

http://www.inkscape.org/ - makes vector images, much higher quality than pixels. I used Inkscape to create the cover for this book. I know it's fairly simple, but it gets the job done and actually took me several hours of watching tutorials to understand what to do. However, I'm no art major, so many of you might be able to use Inkscape to come up with incredible designs from scratch.

(Side note; Inkscape saves most creations as .svg format but it can also save as .pdf. I had to click the Save As a .pdf function, and then download another software to convert it to a .jpeg file which is fairly standard for uploading images like book covers. The conversion program I used is called PDF Xchange Viewer - http://www.pdf-xchange-viewer.en.softonic.com/. Then I opened the PDF Xchange Viewer program, selected my newly created Inkscape .pdf document, under the File tab selected Export and Export to Image, where I could save it as a JPEG image on my desktop and I hit the Export button. It worked great, sounds harder than it is.)

These are also recommended image and graphic editors:

http://www.gimp.org/

http://www.getpaint.net/ - works with Windows only.

http://www.seashore.sourceforge.net/ - works with Mac only.

Now, you should spend some quality time here and come up with a cover design that makes you happy. Remember that it doesn't have to be perfect, but you want it as good as you think it can be. No need to rush through this one.

When you've created a cover design, follow up with action. Take your book cover image and upload it to your blog site; write a blog on how you created it. Share it with your friends on Facebook, and you can even tweet about it asking what others think of your design. You'll probably get a lot of pats on the back, but some people might have excellent suggestions for making it even better. If you do this, the best part is that you'll be engaging your social media and online platform with information about your ebook, which is a good habit to get into.

(And if making a cover turns into an absolute drag, you can find plenty of professional cover designers with a search or via list@smashwords.com. I recommend talking to several, getting quotes and seeing examples of their work.)

After you've created your ebook cover there are some things to know. First, the major websites have a separate upload for the cover as they do for the ebook itself. Other minor sites will just have one upload. So you'll want to have two versions of your ebook with one version where your ebook cover is a separate document. For minor sites that don't have a separate upload for the cover, it's okay to display your cover as the entire first page of your book because that's what will be portrayed in the store of that site. So use the Insert feature of your word processing program to insert the cover image to the first page. Microsoft Word is a great program for everything this ebook talks about. If you don't have it, there's a fairly good, compatible substitute called Open Office (.odt files) that has a free download at http://www.openoffice.org/. You can insert cover images and copy and paste text documents into an Open Office file and work with that. You can view Word Docs with Open Office and even save your files as Word Docs (.doc) by choosing the Save As function and selecting Word Doc (.doc).

And on we go to formatting.

Formatting and Uploading for Smashwords, Amazon and other Retailers

The obvious question is this; *how do I prepare my document to be readable on all those different devices?* Unfortunately, there are several formats that e-reading devices employ. The myriad of these formats is sometimes referred to as "the Tower of eBable." Names include but are not limited to: .txt - plain text, .htm or .html - readable on a web browser, .azw - (Amazon Whispernet) readable on Kindle, .pdf - Adobe Portable Document Format, readable or convertible for almost any device, .pdb - Palm Media, Blackberry and iPhones, .mobi - for Mobipocket and Kindle, .epub - for Sony Reader, Nook, iPad and a host of others now that it's becoming a media standard. Whew! And to think there are a few more.

While you likely have written your book in such documents as Microsoft Word or Works, Mac RTF or other writing program, it's necessary to do conversions to make it ready for at least the majority of e-reading devices. Not to worry, since there is no need to make a dozen conversions for every possible device. The reason is that many owners are already familiar with how to take a .pdf, for example, and convert it to their needs.

The big 4 formats are .pdf, .epub, .mobi and .txt files. They represent 79% of the ebook formats that were downloaded in

January 2010 via Smashwords, which is an ebook retailer that converts files into multiple formats, and a venue where you'll be selling from. (If you really want to add some other formats, .lrf, .rtf, and .pdb represent the sum total of 19% of the rest. Surprisingly, it's hard to find more current stats on this that are reputable.)

For starting out, let's just focus on the big 4: .pdf, .epub, .mobi and .txt. If you can convert your document into these four formats, you'll be fine. (In fact, you really only need to worry about converting to pdf and epub for selling from your own sites since most people that read mobi files are Kindle owners who buy almost exclusively through Amazon. I like having my ebooks available at my sites in mobi too, but I get way more downloads in pdf and some in epub while almost none in mobi.)

In the next chapter, I'm going to give several options on how to convert your documents for sales on your own sites. My advice is to skim through those options and decide which ones are best before trying the very first one. But before I do that, we're going to do something much more fun. It's time to upload to Smashwords, Amazon, Barnes & Noble and other retailers. We're going to discuss the first three individually, as they each have a few specifics that will make the finished product work its best. However, let me make a few common points on how to prepare your document so formatting will go more smoothly on their end, and you'll increase the chance of being accepted by them.

To begin, your documents need to be as simple as possible without a lot of complicated or fancy formatting. For example, e-readers are not like books in that they don't have page numbers, so get rid of page numbers, page references, etc. Here's a quick checklist of things to fix or avoid before attempting to upload to the big retailers:

Don't have large font sizes, nothing over 12 for text and 14 or 16 at the most for the title.

Beware of fancy fonts. Stick to the common ones. Times New Roman. Garamond. Arial. Courier.

Don't use tabs or spaces for indents. Just use the basic settings on the ruler bar: left and right indents for margins, and first line indent for new paragraph placement. Or you can use the block method for a new paragraph with a space of 6pts after a return, which is better than two returns in a row.

Don't have more than 4 consecutive paragraph returns. They can create blank screens of ebook pages, especially on the smaller screens. If you want to show a time lapse within a paragraph, just use a paragraph return followed by three asterisks and another return (or something similar).

Use a manual page break to create a new chapter or text which starts on the next screen, or if you want an image to begin on a new screen. This works great for Amazon Kindle and Smashwords uploads (Smashwords also recommends a paragraph return before and after each manual page break). For Barnes & Noble uploads, use a section break instead of a manual page break to create new chapters or text that goes on a new screen. Fortunately both Amazon and Barnes & Noble have Previews of your upload so you can see what it will look like on a Kindle or Nook before publishing.

Don't include page numbers anywhere. E-reading devices have different screen dimensions and viewers can alter the font size, so page numbers mean nothing to those things.

Don't include images larger than 4 inches in height or width. Resize large pictures to smaller ones to be enjoyed on tiny screens.

For books with a Table of Contents (TOC) and chapter titles, create a manual hyperlink for chapters in the TOC to go to the proper place in the document when clicked (like in this book's beginning at the TOC or when I refer to something like the start of this chapter). Using MS Word, this is done by highlighting the letters for where the chapter begins and selecting Insert then Bookmark and naming it without spaces between words. Return to the TOC and select Insert then Hyperlink then Place in This Document and choose the one you just created. Now try clicking on it from the TOC and see if it zooms instantly to that chapter. Other word processing programs will have a similar method.

Similarly, you can also create NCX files (Navigation Control for XML) by using the words like this, Chapter 1: Example of NCX before the actual place in the text where that chapter starts using those same words, Chapter 1: Example of NCX. Epub file sellers like Barnes & Noble and Apple will create a user-friendly table of contents as a menu option for documents that have this NCX file. My uploads to Amazon just have manual hyperlinks, but my Smashwords uploads also have the NCX files.

A savvy reader might deduce that it's smart to have three slightly different versions of your document: one for Amazon, one for Barnes & Noble and one for Smashwords. That's what I do. The Amazon version has manual page breaks for chapters and a hyperlinked TOC. The Barnes & Noble version has section breaks for chapters. The Smashwords version additionally has an NCX file and the required Smashwords front matter, which is explained in the Style Guide (below).

These are the main points most authors will need, but there are plenty more for specifics. I won't attempt to re-invent the wheel so for super-detailed information on formatting, Mark Coker of Smashwords has written a comprehensive style guide on the subject that can be found at his website - http://smashwords.com. It really is *the authority* on the subject. See the Smashwords **Style Guide** for ebook formatting at http://www.smashwords.com/books/view/52. This will also help dramatically with formatting for other major retailers like Amazon. (If needed, cheap help can be found at Smashwords for both cover design and formatting by sending an email asking for these things to list@smashwords.com. But I prefer learning it since I can make my own changes whenever needed.)

(Side note; most ebook retailers prefer uploads in Microsoft Word .doc or .docx format. In the next chapter I'll explain in more detail for many who don't have this program. Although, even if a computer doesn't have Microsoft Word, many can still utilize the Save As options and save the document as a Word doc. For example, those who have Microsoft Works which is .wps, there is a Save As option to change the file type by clicking the Save As Type box and dragging it down to a .docx, .doc, .html, .rtf, or plain text .txt. Microsoft Works can save files as Word documents; it just can't open and edit in that format. If that's not working, you can always skip ahead to the next chapter on Making Your Own Conversions and formatting for Word .doc and come back here.)

Sometimes authors of certain books (like poetry) have extremely fancy fonts or creative ways of placing the words on the page. In this case, the uploads to retailers may be a challenge to get the intended look. As a solution, some authors create jpeg images of their text, and then upload the images to the screen instead of doing it as straight text. This requires trial and error and checking how results look in the Preview mode at major retailers, but isn't a bad way to go. As the chapter on Cover Design explains, PDF Xchange Viewer can make jpeg images of anything saved as a .pdf file.

Upload to Smashwords.com.

While it's true that Smashwords doesn't have nearly the same market size as Amazon, it's still important for other reasons and a good place to start. Reading through the **Style Guide** may feel like torture at moments, but it's the best way to understand formatting for any possible question, although the highlights that I mentioned above are what most people will need.

What sets Smashwords apart is that they are both a format conversion mechanism and a distributor to many retailers. They convert documents into every format you need plus they get your ebook into some places you wouldn't be able to get into otherwise. No matter what type of e-reading device a potential customer has, Smashwords will create a version of your book to fit the device.

That's really handy. Smashwords also pays authors a whopping 85% of royalties on any Smashwords sale, which is among the best royalties you'll find. Smashwords also distributes its ebooks to multiple online retailers and mobile phone apps. This list of retailers presently includes Barnes & Noble, Apple, Amazon, Sony, Kobo and Diesel, provided your ebook has been accepted in the Premium program, which simply means an ebook is properly formatted and has a quality cover image and ISBN (you can get one freely through Smashwords). Because Smashwords takes a small cut when an ebook sells via Barnes & Noble, for example, it's up to you whether to upload directly to B & N or to opt-in for Smashwords distribution. (I currently do both and have two versions of my books at B & N. So far, this hasn't been a problem.)

Smashwords doesn't encrypt its conversions with DRM (Digital Rights Management.) This way a customer can download an ebook and transfer it from their pc to any device or multiple devices. The customer has more options with the book which is different than the way Amazon presents a book encrypted with DRM, and is only good for one reader's account. Every retailer lets you set and change your price, but Smashwords also allows you to enable sample chapters for customers to browse as much of the book as you'd like them to (a good way to hook readers), and they also have coupons which can be set for any amount. The only current cons to Smashwords are a limited customer base compared to Amazon and that some customers complain downloading is more difficult. But these things could change in time and Smashwords does have plenty of positives.

You'll need to read the Smashwords Style Guide, which isn't long, as it's the best way to understand how to format your document before uploading (*something that will help with uploading to any retailer*). The tips I gave you earlier are the majority of them, but the Style Guide goes into far more detail. Microsoft Word .doc files work the best for uploading, and then .rtf files are second best. (In the next chapter I'll cover plenty of options for converting formats yourself if you need to figure this out.) Once you've followed the Style Guide completely, upload your book by following the Publishing prompts. Take some time and write a thoughtful description that will help readers identify the content of your ebook and decide to buy. (Save the description in your folder also, as you'll be using it often.) Remember, a good cover image is needed to be eligible for the Premium program which gets you into many other retailers. But not to worry, if for some reason they deny you, just make alterations and try again.

The other great thing about uploading to Smashwords is that you'll have to format your ebook correctly in accordance with their Style Guide. Assuming you pass that test, your ebook will more likely be accepted by Amazon and it will look good on Kindle readers.

How well do ebooks sell on Smashwords? There's a broad range. Some sell hardly at all while others sell over a thousand units per month. It depends on the quality of the story and writing, the degree to which the author markets wisely, markets persistently and a slew of other factors. I don't sell nearly as many ebooks through Smashwords as I do from my own websites and from Amazon, but that's not a big deal. Because of the additional benefits, that Smashwords makes multiple format conversions and gets me into every other retailer, that's why it's mandatory to also sell with them.

(Remember if you need to make edits or additions later, you can simply upload a new version to replace the old one. This is true for most any ebook retailer and a bonus factor that makes e-publishing very attractive compared to print.)

For more information and to get your ebooks for sale on Smashwords visit - http://www.smashwords.com.

Amazon.com.

Amazon is the world's largest bookseller and a must for any author with an ebook. Your book can be uploaded and placed in their Kindle program for free, and Amazon will convert your book to .azw/.mobi format to be read by its Kindle readers. Just go to https://kdp.amazon.com/mn/signin where you'll be asked to create an Amazon account if you don't already have one. Then follow their guidelines for uploading your ebook, cover and description. Amazon recommends uploading in Microsoft Word .doc format, or .html or .prc. You can also use programs like MobiPocket Creator and Amazon's free Kindle Previewer, but I haven't found them to be necessary as my MS Word .doc uploads work fine and they have a built in Previewer when uploading. As a last resort .pdf files can be uploaded but they caution against poor conversion quality. Since they do have a Preview button, what it will look like on a Kindle, you can try the .pdf option and see if it works before getting locked in. (Again, I'll cover formatting in the next chapter for those who don't have Microsoft Word or need help making the conversion.) The same book description from Smashwords can be used or it can be altered. During the uploading process, you can set the price and later change it if that's something you decide to do. As of this writing, Amazon offers a 70% royalty per sale to authors provided you have the book priced between $2.99 and $9.99 and don't have it anywhere for cheaper than on Amazon. Other price points just pay 35%. There are a few other limitations that can be found at kdp.amazon.com.

Amazon has a box to check if you want the cover image added to the beginning of the Kindle version. I check this box and do not include the cover image in my document when uploading so the cover image won't be duplicated at the start.

You can also add a bookmark for the Table of Contents and where you prefer a Kindle reader to Start the book (from their menu options) by using these bookmarks respectively, *toc* and *start*. Employ them by placing the cursor at the beginning of the TOC, for example, select Insert then Boomark then type *toc* and Add.

As of Dec. 2011, Amazon introduced a new program called KDP Select. By enrolling in the program, the author agrees not to make her/his ebook available *anywhere else other than Amazon* for a period of at least 90 days. The author gains access to Amazon's Kindle Owner Lending Library and is eligible for extra bonus money depending on the amount of "borrows" the book receives. More information is here - https://kdp.amazon.com/self-publishing/help?topicId=A6KILDRNSCOBA. That being said, **I do not participate** in the KDP Select program since I like selling ebooks from every retailer possible and my own websites. However, this is a personal choice. If you would like to only target Amazon Kindle, which represents the majority of my sales, this choice could simplify your efforts tremendously. The downside is that you can't provide your book anywhere else, whether at another retailer or even your own website.

Also know that once any book is live on Amazon, it can have tags added. Tags can be inserted by both authors and browsers. They work like search engine terms to help customers find specific books without having to scroll through millions of titles. For example, the tags for this book include: sell ebooks, e-publishing, ebook business, publish ebooks, online marketing, self publish, writers and more, all of which will lead some browsers to my book using the Search for Products Tagged With function. Any person can add 15 tags per book. Over time, these can really add up and help customers find a title with a tag search, so be sure to leave lots of tags on the product page.

Amazon also has an Author Central division that will help you make the very most of your experience there. Obviously, Amazon wants you to sell as many books as possible and will do whatever they can to help. https://authorcentral.amazon.com/gp/landing

(Side note; a question that many authors ask is *how much to charge for their ebook*. This is a personal choice and varies greatly depending on the type of book and the length. However, a couple of things seem obvious to me. First of all, ebooks should be substantially less expensive than paper books since they cost nearly nothing to produce. A big trend is moving towards cheaper and cheaper ebooks even though traditional publishers are going to war with Amazon over maintaining high prices like $14.99, although it amazes me how many ebooks are either free or extremely cheap, like 99 cents. A second thought is that gaining readership and building a name for a new author might be more important than trying to get a few extra bucks. It could be worthwhile to sell an ebook for 99 cents if it means selling a few hundred or even a few thousand copies quickly and getting your name and book out there. Once people are happily recommending it and sales/reviews are established, you can always raise the price and see how that goes. Some 99 cent authors, like Darcie Chan of *The Mill River Recluse*, have made it to the top of Amazon sales by pricing low and marketing aggressively. I plan on selling this ebook for $4.99 to start even though I know it has tremendous value. I believe this ebook could sell for much more because it will save the customers a huge amount of time, money and effort with the advice. Other ebooks I researched like this were charging up to $50 and more. Is this ebook worth $15, $25, even $50 or more because of the value within? Of course it is, but pricing it there at the onset might discourage a lot of buyers and delay its progress and potential.)

Barnes & Noble.

When I first wrote this book in March of 2010, B & N wasn't an option for direct uploading. It had to be done via Smashwords. Now you can with their Pubit program. Just visit the site and follow the prompts as it's a very similar process to the others.

The main difference I've experienced with Pubit uploads as compared to kdp.amazon, is that manual page breaks don't work the same to create new chapters or text on a new screen. Instead of manual page breaks, I use section breaks to create new chapters for B & N. Make sure to see how it looks in the Preview mode.

The other difference I've seen is that images come out smaller on the Pubit Preview than they do on the Kindle Preview. Don't ask me why, but I'm able to use slightly larger images for Barnes &

Noble uploads than for Amazon, even though the Kindle and Nook have screens the same size.

Otherwise, the process is virtually identical. It's a real blessing to be able to scroll through the Previews of your upload to see how things will look before publishing.

http://pubit.barnesandnoble.com/

Apple iBookstore.

This is one I haven't done personally as I don't have a Mac (one of the many requirements from Apple to self-publish with them) and all of my books were already on the site via Smashwords before they allowed direct uploading. It's done through an application process at this link - https://itunesconnect.apple.com/WebObjects/iTunesConnect.wo a/wa/apply. My apologies for not having more specifics on this, but I assume it's very similar to the others, except the application process. If you don't have a Mac or are not accepted by Apple, just get into the iBookstore via Smashwords.

Google Ebooks.

This came out in January 2011 and was originally going to be called Google Editions. Dumb name, I know. I've recently uploaded with them but haven't experienced hardly any sales yet. A few sales have happened and some small change from AdWords revenue, which is nice. I recommend them even though I have doubts and issues. It should be noted that they just recently partnered up with a dedicated reader, the Story HD by iRiver . While Kindle, Nook and iPad owners are far more likely to buy ebooks from Amazon, B & N and Apple respectively, who are the big buyers for Google Ebooks? I just don't believe the iRiver will ever truly compete with these other established brands, and only time will tell.

The method of uploading with them is quite similar, although it takes up to several weeks for ebooks to "process" and actually show up with a search at their Ebookstore. It also seems nearly impossible to make any edits after uploading or to get decent customer support. I believe they're still working on some bugs so maybe by the time you upload it will be streamlined. You need a Google account to sign up for their Partner Program, which is all free of course. At the time of this writing, I consider Google Ebooks as a place for extra visibility but not really for sales. That could change in time.

https://books.google.com/partner

The following sites you may consider optional. In my opinion, the more places you have your ebook for sale the better. But the places that are mandatory are Smashwords, Amazon, Barnes & Noble, Apple and your own sites, which we'll discuss soon. The next sites are supplemental and good, yet not nearly as important.

Scribd.com.

They're another outfit, and you'll find the process very much like uploading with Amazon or Smashwords. The main difference with Scribd is that they don't convert your work into other formats. Scribd accepts Word Docs, PDF, PowerPoint and Excel formats and makes them available for viewing. I believe many Scribd users read on their computer screens, but some of these people also know how to convert any document to be readable on an e-reading device, so don't be surprised to find someone reading your Scribd upload on their iPhone. Again, you can name your price with Scribd, but the vast majority of the documents there are for free. Sales here will be a lot harder to come by. *A smart thing to do with Scribd is to upload a third (33%) of your ebook at no charge with links at the end for where to buy it if they want to keep reading*. My books have been read thousands of times this way, like a sampling, and I believe some of those reads have resulted in sales at places like Amazon.

Also you should note with Scribd that there is no separate cover upload, so the first page of your document will act as your cover. In this case you'll want the cover image to be full page.

Scribd also allows people to subscribe to you, which is sort of like Twitter and followers. It helps to subscribe back to those who do because it puts your face on their subscriber list so others can find you. http://www.scribd.com/

Youpublish.com.

This site belongs to Mark Victor Hansen, a major player in the publishing industry. He co-authored the *Chicken Soup* series, runs Mega Book Marketing seminars and appears genuinely dedicated to helping independent authors get their books out in the public. You'll find the process here very similar to Scribd and Myebook (below). Again, sales will be a lot harder to come by than on Amazon and Smashwords, but often the important thing is getting readers checking out your book and clicking your links.

http://youpublish.com/

MyEbook.com.

This is a fairly new site. It probably has a similar reader base to Scribd and, like them, will be harder to generate sales but another place to get people reading your book. After registering you can upload your book in PDF format through their ebook builder, which is a user friendly drag and drop method of putting a package together. The ebook viewer for completed projects actually looks like a three dimensional book on a computer screen with pages turning in an aesthetically pleasing display. Viewers also have interactive options such as leaving comments on certain pages, so it's good for photo albums or books with lots of images. They also have a book cover design and the ability to embed links to videos, audio, documents, images and flash files to make your books fully interactive. Like the others, you can sell and name your price. As with Scribd, it might be smart to offer 30% to 50% of your ebooks here with links at the end for those who want to buy it. Find more information at http//www.myebook.com.

eBay is an outfit I will discuss in the Cheating With Money Chapter, because listing a product there does cost money. However, I have sold some ebooks there, so definitely consider them as a possibility.

Other sites for retailing ebooks are popping up everyday. The field is growing exponentially, faster than most any other industry, so don't be surprised if you find other options than the ones I've listed. In some ways, this is like social media where the more sites you're listed on the better. And yet, as long as your ebook is listed on the biggies like Amazon, B & N, Apple and Smashwords, that's fine. I usually just offer samples at the other sites with links at the end for buyers.

Follow up with action. Once your ebook is available on Amazon, Smashwords and any other retailer, the things to do are to use your blog and social media sites to make an announcement and post links to them. Everywhere you announce its presence, include the link page for the retailer where it can be found. Make a post on Amazon Kindle Meet Our Authors forum in threads for new book releases (you can also insert links directly to your ebook there). Contact sites that specialize in your genre and post there. Email friends and family with the links and ask them to pass it on and click on your tags. Share your links with Facebook friends and groups. Make Google Plus announcements. Let others know it's available, a bit about the story and how it can help or entertain them. Keep it engaging without sounding boastful, and hopefully readers will come to the ebook to purchase it.

The free option.
It's not a bad way to go if your primary intent is to build a readership base. Many authors get hundreds to thousands of

downloads every week that their book is available for free. Maybe once a following of readers is established, then you can start charging and take your ebooks off the free sites. The minor problem of having your ebook on these sites is that free ebooks often get shared with other sites and you might discover them floating around Cyberspace and have to chase down a few webmasters. (Google Alerts is extremely helpful for catching and stopping this, as I've done plenty of times. Just set a Google Alert for your book's title and you'll know if someone has posted it.)

That being said, in the past I placed my novels on some free sites and had tremendous benefits. In a few months I had over 10,000 downloads from people all over the world. I also received nearly a dozen unsolicited comments and reviews from grateful readers, some of which turned into testimonials that I could use on my blog and websites as book reviews. Plus, after 10,000 downloads, it felt good thinking there was a strong chance somebody somewhere was reading my words. I just liked knowing that.

There are literally dozens of websites to download free ebooks, which means all of these sites also accept free ebooks. Just check out their sites, see what the submission policies are and decide if you want to do it. Here are a few of them, and again, this is a partial list:

http://www.bookbuzzr.com/ - creates a flappable book cover design for interactive browsing.

http://www.freado.com/

http://www.free-ebooks.net/

http://www.getfreeebooks.com/

Ultimately, the best royalties from the sale of your ebook is through your own website. Some of you may have a site already (especially those who moved forward with Wordpress or Blogger), others may not. Either way, I'd like to cover the basics of selling your book through both your blog site and your website, which you can have for free.

But before we do, let's talk about manually converting your documents to multiple e-readable formats.

Formatting for Your Sites, Making Your own Conversions

(Side note; here's a brief mention on converting Microsoft Works (.wps) to other formats. Some PC owners may only have their factory included word processing program, Microsoft Works (.wps files). It's not a very compatible format and necessary to convert into at least one other format, then use that to switch to the rest. There are a couple of ways to do this. The easiest way is to use the Save As option, and then select the file type to .rtf, .doc or some other format. Then you can use the below programs to convert it further. You can also either download file converters or work directly through Microsoft, which has free downloads and tutorials that help convert versions or Works - http://office.microsoft.com/en-us/word/HP011881161033.aspx. And there's also Microsoft support for more options - http://support.microsoft.com/. A final resort is saving a Works document as plain text. You'll lose the formatting which would have to be replaced in another program, like Open Office, but at least conversions would be easier from there.)

Let's get back to the big 4 formats. Here's a quick review of each:

1. PDF, Portable Document Format from Adobe, represents the format for about 35% of ebook downloads. PDF has long been the number one format partly because it's been around since 1993 and was officially declared an open standard in 2008. *This is by far the main format people choose when they download directly from my websites.* It's also a good format for charts, images and fancy formatting but not the best for straight narrative. Conversions are freely available from every other format. I'll give you a list of places to convert documents to PDF format for free, but you can always Google "convert (fill in your word program here) to PDF" for more options.

(An important note on Microsoft Word .doc or .docx; if you have a recent version of Microsoft Word, then you can create your own PDFs. Just open your document and go to the Save As tab. When you utilize Save As, one of the options will be PDF. Click on that and *shazam,* you've just published a .pdf version of your document. If that's not an option, try going to one of these sites and making a free conversion.)

http://www.pdfonline.com/convert-pdf/ - no download needed. Converts most any document and most images (like .jpeg) to PDF. It works super easy by just browsing a document to upload, giving your email address and waiting one minute for it to arrive.

http://www.freepdfconvert.com/ - no download needed. Converts Word, Open Office, Lotus, images and other formats to PDF. Required to wait 30 minutes in between multiple conversions.

http://www.calibre-ebook.com/- download required but **Calibre is an amazing tool and can handle most (if not all) of your conversion needs.** It also acts as an e-reading device that can check any format that your computer might otherwise not be able to open. Don't have a Kindle or a Nook or an iPad but want to know what your conversion would look like on them? Calibre will show you. *For those reasons, I **highly recommend it as a somewhat*** *mandatory item.* **Calibre converts most any format (except Word** .doc) to PDF, Epub, Mobi and to most any other format. (Word Docs can be saved as html or other formats and then Calibre will work. But we'll also cover a great way to convert Word to Epub in a moment with 2epub.com, as Calibre likes working with Epub.)

From Calibre's website, *Input Formats:* CBZ, CBR, CBC, EPUB, FB2, HTML, LIT, LRF, MOBI, ODT, PDF, PRC, PDB, PML, RB, RTF, TCR and TXT.

Output Formats: EPUB, FB2, OEB, LIT, LRF, MOBI, PDB, PML, RB, PDF, TCR and TXT.

What are the best source formats to convert? In order from preferred to decreasing preference: LIT, MOBI, EPUB, HTML, PRC, RTF, PDB, TXT and PDF.

Why does PDF conversion lose some images/tables? The PDF conversion tries to extract the text and images from the PDF file and convert them to an HTML based ebook. Some PDF files have images in a format that cannot be extracted (vector images, like what Inkscape creates). All tables are also represented as vector diagrams, thus they cannot be extracted. That being said, I've uploaded .pdf files to Calibre and easily converted to .epub and .mobi. The files and my two images came out beautifully, so it may be all you need unless you have lots of images, graphs and/or vectors.

In a nutshell, Calibre allows you to upload documents and Add them to a Library. From there you can do many things including Convert Ebooks to multiple formats as well as save them to destination folders and View them. It's a great tool for accomplishing many of your goals here and much more. There's a demo video at Calibre and some on YouTube. There's also an owner's manual with an FAQ section at http://calibre-ebook.com/user_manual/.

http://www.doc2pdf.net/ - download required. Converts Word to PDF.

http://www.primopdf.com/index.aspx - download required. Converts Word, Excel, and PowerPoint to PDF.

Again, there are other options if you use a search engine to find a free conversion tool for your particular writing program.

2. EPUB, electronic publication, is a free and open ebook standard by the International Digital Publishing Forum that has recently been named the new industry standard. Epub is designed for reflowable content which means the text can be altered or optimized for any particular reading device. It's great for straight narrative but not the best for certain layouts or advanced formatting such as comic books or technical books with lots of graphs. Epub can be read by Barnes & Noble's Nook, Sony Readers, Apple's iPad, tablets and a host of other devices which clearly makes Epub a very important format to have. Epub files made up 22% of ebook downloads via Smashwords (Jan 2010), but with the addition of Apple's iPad and other tablets that number is likely to change dramatically.

(For those who don't have an Epub reading device like Nook or Sony Reader, and for some reason can't use Calibre as I mentioned above, you can download software as a Firefox Add-on called EpubReader that allows you to read and save .epub files. Here's how; upload Mozilla Firefox as your internet web browser. Some people might raise an eyebrow to uploading a new web browser, but Firefox is excellent and many insist it's the best web browser. I switched from Internet Explorer and absolutely love Firefox. Download Firefox at http://www.mozilla.com/en-US/firefox/personal.html. Once that's done, this Add-on will read .epub files - https://addons.mozilla.org/en-US/firefox/addon/45281. Then you can open an .epub file from the webpage it's on or from your computer by clicking on it, choose the program to Open With and click the Browse button which will list Firefox as an option to open it with. Then you can view .epub files, including the ones you'll end up creating. Like Calibre, this is a handy tool for checking your conversions later.)

To convert your document to .epub, follow the same advice as you did for .pdf. I will present several websites for free conversions, but you may also Google the phrase, "convert (fill in your word program here) to Epub" for more options.

http://www.2epub.com/ - no download required, really an **awesome conversion tool that I highly recommend.** Converts Word .doc (not .docx), .fb2, .html, .lit, .lrf, .mobi, .odt, .pdb, .pdf, .prc, .rtf, .txt to .epub, .mobi, .lrf and other formats in 3 steps. Browse the document to choose, click Upload Files and leave your Title and Author name on Auto or name them if you want, Convert Files to Epub, then right click to save it, Save As Link and choose your "ebooksuccess" folder. Repeat the process to Convert to Other Formats such as Mobi. Notice that it doesn't work with .docx, Word's most recent version. The simple fix if you have .docx is to Save As a Word Document or a Word 97-2003 Document which will be a .doc file. It's limited to files 25MB in size, which is actually over ten times larger than both of my novels combined. If you have an enormous file to convert with tons of images, 2epub.com recommends Calibre.

http://www.calibre-ebook.com/ - as I explained above, this is mandatory software to download. Calibre converts most any format (except Word .doc) to Epub, Mobi and most any other format. Plus it does so much more that I highly recommend it.

http://epub2go.com/ - no download required. Converts PDF to Epub.

http://www.bookdesigner.org/ - converts Word, .pdf, .rtf, .txt, and most other formats to .epub, .mobi and other formats. It's similar to Calibre but not as clean to the eye or quite as user-friendly in my opinion, although it does receive Word Docs. However, I lost some of my spacing when I converted a .doc file to .mobi as a test, so that was a small concern. (Note; this is a Russian website so you'll probably need to translate the page. If you Google "bookdesigner," there will be a result that says - http://www.bookdesigner.org. That will also have a tab to the right that says Translate This Page. Hit the Translate button and view it in English. Once downloaded, it's an easy switch from Russian to English with a button in the upper left.)

3. MOBI, for mobile devices that can access the web, .mobi is the file type read by Amazon Kindle and Mobipocket devices. It's also used for PDA, Smartphone, Blackberry, Palm devices and some others. Mobi format represents 15% of electronic downloads via Smashwords and 100% of Amazon Kindle downloads. Here are some options for converting your documents to .mobi files.

http://www.calibre-ebook.com/ - if you haven't read my paragraphs from before then see them now.

http://www.mobipocket.com/en/downloadSoft/ProductDetailsCreator.asp - converts, Word, .html, .pdf, and .txt files to .mobi.

http://www.bookdesigner.org/ - converts Word, .pdf, .rtf, .txt, and most other formats to .epub, .mobi and other formats. It's similar to Calibre, see my comments above.

Besides Calibre, another program for viewing .mobi files is Amazon's Kindle for PC. It only works for files that Kindles can read, but it's a valuable tool for checking your conversions and is free - http://www.amazon.com/gp/kindle/pc. To view a .mobi file after downloading it (or something that says Kindle Content), just right click on the document icon, then Open With and choose the Amazon Kindle for PC Application.

Again, if these options aren't working for you, use a search engine for more.

4. Plain Text or .txt format. This is the most easily read format that works on almost every screen and accounts for 9% of electronic downloads via Smashwords (Jan. 2010). Because of their simplicity, virtually every writing program has the option to save a document as a plain text file, .txt. It lacks formatting but works everywhere. For best results with plain text, source documents

77

shouldn't contain images or fancy formatting. Just open your Save As tab and scroll through the options until you find a Plain Text or .txt option. Or you can right click over a blank spot on your Desktop and choose the New option and then the Text Document tab. When you create and view a Text document you may need to hit the Format tab and choose Word Wrap to get the page to look proper without the lines running horizontally forever. If that's not working, then go through one of the options above for multi-purpose formatting like Calibre. It's also not very good for certain things like *italics* or **bold** as it seems to be an all or nothing case with many computers, so consider using Plain Text just as a back-up.

Okay, now you have a plethora of free options for converting your documents to e-documents in multiple formats. What next? Checking the work is smart. Somehow you need to see if the conversions worked for the devices they are meant to be viewed on. Here are a few ways to do this:

Easiest way— inspect your documents on Calibre since Calibre can view all of the formats that e-readers can view. If they look like you want them to look, then they're probably okay. You can also view your .mobi files on Amazon Kindle for PC in the method described above. You can view the .epub files in the Firefox EpubReader described above.

Next easiest way— if you own any e-reading devices or have a friend that owns one, a Nook for example, then download the .epub file via a USB cable and see how it looks on the Nook. If it looks great, you're done. Try viewing it on an iPhone if you have access to one with an e-reading application. If the document needs adjusting, then figure that out and make alterations. Hopefully it won't need too many fixes because you've likely already uploaded with Amazon and Smashwords, and they wouldn't have accepted it unless it was pretty good. (If this is the case and you're concerned about those uploads, not to worry. It's never too late to edit your version or completely delete it and upload a new one. It might take a couple of days to see your new version on Amazon, but at least it will be as you like.) Do this physical check for as many devices as possible for .pdf, .mobi and the .epub files.

Medium hard way— go online to Facebook or any other social network and ask for volunteers to look at your e-book on their devices for free. Facebook has groups for all different types of e-readers which are easy to find with a Facebook Group Search. You can make a post asking people to download the files you need tested to their device via a USB cable and let you know how it looks. They'll be getting a free ebook and you'll be getting valuable feedback.

Final way— take your chances and run with it. I've done this and then simply visited the nearest Apple store, for example, and checked my book's sample while browsing iPads. If someone purchases the book from your site and mentions they can't read it, you'll have an idea of what to change. You'll obviously want to do it right away and be super courteous to the customer. I hope this won't happen, but it is a possibility and wouldn't be the end of the world.

The tools exist to convert your books into multiple e-formats as well as those to create your own covers. Once you've got these two things mastered, you'll be creating ebooks for your own websites. Now it's time for another step, uploading to your blog and website. Some of you may want to skip ahead to the discussion on uploading files while those without a website may want to read this next part on making one for free.

Creating Your Website

The whole point of having a blog and/or a website is to enhance your online visibility. These sites can say volumes about the author and her/his books, much more than can be accomplished with a mere retailer's page. They can contain sample chapters, display photos and/or video and also link to all of the retail places for sale (like Amazon) as well as your social media sites (like Facebook). My websites lead perfect strangers from all over the world directly to my ebooks and paperbacks. They also help build my social media presence. Without the blogs and websites, it would be a real struggle to acquire readers. Besides having a blog, which I believe is mandatory, you'll benefit greatly from also having a website.

Why? Because it will be a showcase for your book and, once in place, it will take little time to maintain. Your blog site will be dynamic and change regularly while your website will be fairly static. One analogy that comes to mind is that your blog site is like your kitchen; it's the heart center of your home that is continuously being used and brought into minor disarray and cleaned up, with lots of visitors and the potentials for their inputs. Your website is more like a seldom used formal dining room; it changes shape far less often and everything is usually in its place. The other thing is this; your blog also acts as a billboard, an advertising force that directs traffic not only to itself but to your website and the links to retailers. So the short answer is yes, you can have just a blog if you want. But why not add that extra element and also have a website, especially when it's free?

Again, there are dozens of options. Unless you know a lot about building websites, you're also going to want a free site that comes with a user-friendly site-building program. Although there are multiple free website hosting venues, I'm going to stick with ones that also have site-building tools that are easy to use. To be of note, the most common complaints with free websites are that the domain name is followed by the name of the hosting company and there are sometimes paid ads that run on part of the page. Ultimately, if that stuff is a major issue you can upgrade to a paid program for hosting which is generally inexpensive. But to start, I recommend building a free website before making any conversions. I've also written another book that goes into far greater detail on this one element of making free websites and blogs and can be seen at http://your-own-free-website.webs.com. Here are the places I recommend building your site, with the two at the top being my favorites and the others with great reviews:

Webs.com. (Note; there is also a web.com and these are two entirely different entities.)

Webs.com, formerly FreeWebs.com, is easy to use and can help you get a site up and running in just a few hours. I really like Webs.com and found the site-building program very simple to get comfortable with. It's not quite as easy as Yola (which I'll explain next), but its design is similar. If you can handle Microsoft Word, you can use the Webs site-builder program. There's a thorough eight minute video which explains the whole process. They have over 300 premade templates that can be customized to fit your needs, or one can be uploaded if you have something else in mind. It's already designed to help make most of the pages you'll likely want: home, about, photo gallery, online store with built-in PayPal, member's page, guestbook, links and much more. And with all these sites, you can name the individual pages anything you want. They're just giving suggestions. You can also make "hidden" pages that don't show up on the navigation bar (something I'll explain the usefulness later when we're using PayPal and creating Download pages for your ebook). Webs.com allows you many benefits: upload files, photos, use widgets, video, flash, just about anything you'd want in a professional looking website, plus you get ample space for file storage and your own email.

Webs.com currently gives you about 50MB of storage space and a bandwidth capacity of 500MB. To put some perspective on that, everything a visitor clicks on or downloads depletes your monthly bandwidth. Pictures, files, etc, things that get clicked on all slowly reduce your monthly allotment of bandwidth resource. So if you have some images that are a few hundred K of data and an ebook that is about 1MB (or 1,000K) of data, then those images and that ebook can probably be viewed and downloaded about 300 times in one month before your site would crash from heavy traffic. (Of course, this wouldn't be a problem because if that much business is happening you can always upgrade to their very affordable Premium Starter Package at $5/month which boosts your capacity by ten times. In fact, if at any time your site crashes from heavy traffic, you'll not only want it back online asap but you can open a bottle of champagne as you upgrade!) An easy way to check where you're at with storage and bandwidth is by clicking the Site Settings tab which has a bar graph of Site Usage.

Webs.com also supports all of the files needed to sell ebooks: .pdf, .epub and .mobi. This is extremely handy as you need a site for that even if it's just for storage. Technically, you could market and sell ebooks from Wordpress alone, but your customers would need to be sent to a site like Webs.com to download the product since Wordpress does not support .epub or .mobi files. (Although .pdf files represent well over 90% of customer downloads from my sites, so it could be all you need.)

They do run an ad on the sidebar for the free package, which I find worse that having no ads like at Yola (below), but not a deal breaker because of the ample storage and bandwidth. You can play around with different template choices as some require less ad space than others (I like the Clean Splash template for smaller ads, others might be even better). They also have free stats monitoring, but it's through another company, StatCounter.com - http://my.statcounter.com/register.php, and the process of inserting the stat counter is much like creating a badge widget.

Knowing information about your visitors is hugely important for many reasons. Data like where people are linking from to find you and number of visitors is really useful. StatCounter will also be needed as a safeguard against piracy later when you sell ebooks from a Webs.com (or other) site and want to know how many people besides you have been to your Download page where you provide your ebooks. (I'll explain this all in detail later, though it's good to get it set up now.) StatCounter will tell you your own IP address, and you can double check it here - http://www.whatismyip.com/ or by Googling another website for this. Then as you set up StatCounter, click on My Projects link upper left, click the small wrench icon, click the Edit Settings link, paste your IP Address in the box provided (StatCounter should know your IP Address already and display it to the left) and check the box below saying you want that for all your projects, click Edit Project and it's done. (This will be especially handy when we create your download page.) Then you'll need to Configure and Install the code by following the prompts, which works just like installing an html code widget into the body of text at the bottom of the pages where you want stats counted.

Now, I've taken the liberty of creating an example website for the purpose of this lesson and ebook. You can find it at http://www.ebooksuccess4free.webs.com. I sell many ebooks directly at this site with a system that runs on autopilot. You can see my StatCounter icon at the bottom of my Home page (which will count your visit) and if you could see my Hidden Download page, you'd see it there too. Notice that I don't have it in the sidebar of every page because I only care about the Home and Hidden Download pages, and I want separate stats for those.

This example website serves the purpose of giving you layout ideas that might be helpful but aren't mandatory. Perhaps you'll come up with better ideas on your own. Unfortunately, the sidebar to the right only has preprogrammed and limited widgets for Twitter and some other places, but not Facebook and LinkedIn. So I had to add those badges as Custom Modules in the Sidebar Editing section as html Text widgets, similar to the Badge process from the Social Media section. The Sidebar must be "turned on," and you can also add your own Twitter Module this way if you don't like their limited choices. The free version at Webs also requires you to be at the site for a week before you can receive email notifications from a Contact page.

Check out Webs.com and see if it feels right for you. If it does, it will be handy for much of the rest of my advice which follows, especially as I'll be using Webs.com as my main example to explain things. But if you use another great venue, as I'll show some others below, not to worry. These things are primarily universal, so my advice for Webs will likely work anywhere.

http://www.webs.com/

Yola.com.

I really like Yola and hear a lot of satisfied customers who built sites at Yola.com, formerly called Synthasite and based in San Francisco. It's extremely user-friendly, simple to get familiar with. I built an example for another book that is strictly on creating free websites at http://yourownfreewebsite.yolasite.com and feel very confident recommending them from my experience plus the reviews out there. If you visit the site you'll notice I spent a few bucks for the custom domain name, http://your-own-free-website.com. If you click on the former, it automatically redirects to the latter so people will arrive there either way. This is what the company says about Yola;

With Yola, if you can edit a document, you can build a free website. Yola's award-winning support team is always available, making websites easy to manage and simple to change. Yola packages include over 100 ad-free customizable templates, so you can create a website you'll love without annoying pop-ups. Yola gives you the features you want, including integration with YouTube, Google Maps, and PayPal. With Yola, you'll get up to five free websites with 1GB of storage so you can claim your rightful place on the web. You can purchase your own custom domain name, or decide to use a subdomain that comes with the free website hosting Yola provides. Yola's award-winning support team is always available to not only walk you through the steps to make a free website, but also to provide tips and tricks for making your website stand out and give you a website you're proud of.

What I like about Yola is the lack of a forced ad and the extra storage space. 1GB (gigabyte) of storage is a lot, especially for those who have ample amounts of video and/or audio to present. Drag and drop features make it incredibly easy for anyone to build the pages. They also have a Properties tab on each page for Keywords and SEO tools, a great support staff and forum of helpful people. Additionally for those who really want a free site including AdSense by Google for extra income potential, then Yola would be a great choice.

http://www.yola.com/

Here are some others and there are plenty more:
Weebly - http://www.weebly.com/
Wix - http://www.wix.com/
Jimdo - http://www.jimdo.com/
Webstarts - http://webstarts.com/
Google Sites - https://sites.google.com/

Wordpress.com.

I know we talked about them as a great blog tool, but a site like Wordpress (or Blogger) simply doesn't have to change as frequently. In other words, you can use your blog as a static website. And with 3GB of free storage space, you'll doubtfully need more unless you're posting massive amounts of audio or video. Plus you may already be experienced working with them, and their traffic monitoring stats are extremely useful, the best I've found and included for free. Finally, Wordpress probably has the best search engine optimization with Google.

One downside to having a site only with Wordpress is that it doesn't accept certain formats like .mobi and .epub files. *This is only a downside if you want to sell directly from your site in multiple formats.* Remember the supported files list - http://en.support.wordpress.com/accepted-filetypes/. On the other hand, well over 90% of the downloads directly from my websites are in pdf format, which is supported by Wordpress. Additionally, I sell far more books from retailers like Amazon than from my own sites, but I admit the extra sales are worth the effort. If you wanted to use your Wordpress (or other) blog alone and wanted to have epub and mobi as format options, it would be necessary to link to another site (like Yola or Webs) just for the product download. That actually isn't as much work as it sounds.

http://www.wordpress.com/

Follow up with action. Just as you did after creating a blog, make sure you add your social media badges and the retailer links for your ebook to your website as soon as it's created. You can always add and perfect the individual pages later, but you'll benefit by getting those contact links up right away. Also return to Amazon, Smashwords, Facebook, Twitter, LinkedIn, etc and add your new website's URL to your profile assuming it has space for more than one URL. Click on those links to make sure they work. If a site only allows one URL (like Amazon) then decide which one you'd prefer.

There is a second way to create your website, by using a hosting company that doesn't provide site-building software. One can be built and designed entirely from scratch if you're a bit adventurous and computer savvy. There are literally dozens of free hosting sites that don't offer site-building programs. Instead they just offer the hosting while you create and provide all the website content. If manually creating a website from scratch is something you'd like to do, there is a free download for software called Kompozer. Kompozer is fairly easy to use (as far as web-designing software goes), making it ideal for non-technical computer users who want to create an attractive, professional-looking website without needing to know HTML or web coding. It employs WYSIWYG web page editing. It is user friendly but not nearly as easy as the Yola or Webs.com site-building programs. I've used Kompozer and can vouch for its simplicity, but you'll need an instruction booklet or video to go along with it. Kompozer can be downloaded from http://www.kompozer.net/.

If you're going to try using Kompozer, then I recommend reading this free tutorial by Chris Farrell called *Create Your Own Website By 3:45 This Afternoon.* It's a great .pdf ebook that takes you step by step through building a website with Kompozer. I had to Google "free ebooks Chris Farrell" to find it, so you can too if this link isn't working in the future - http://www.free-ebooks.net/authors.php?author=Chris%20Farrell.

Remember, there are tons of companies that offer free hosting, so here's a brief list of web hosting companies that do not offer site-building tools:

http://www.50Webs.com/ - no forced ads, unlimited bandwidth.

http://www.awardspace.com/ - no forced ads, 5GB/month bandwidth.

http://www.leadhoster.com/ - top banner ads, 5 GB/month bandwidth.

http://www.host-ed.net/ - no forced ads, 5 GB/month bandwidth.

http://www.tekcities.com/ - no forced ads, 5 GB/month bandwidth.

Okay, before I talk about selling your ebook from your own websites, I'd like to cover SEO (Search Engine Optimization) in the next chapter. The reason is because SEO takes time. *Climbing to the top of the rankings will not be an instantaneous leap but will happen slowly and surely.* From the time that you submit your sites to the search engines, plus your social media links, plus your blog comments and everywhere to get your URLs out there… it will still take several weeks to a few months before real results happen. We'll discuss getting that ball rolling with SEO, and then we can cover selling your ebook. Also, I have written an entire book dedicated to SEO tips, which I only have space here to briefly mention. For those who want much more on the subject, please see *Get On Google Front Page* at any retailer or at http://getongooglefrontpage.webs.com/.

SEO (Search Engine Optimization)

Another highly important element in optimizing your online platform and internet presence is maximizing the ability of search engines like Google, Yahoo and Bing to find you. There are many ways to help in this regard, ***but remember that this takes time.*** Most search engine indexes/directories update themselves monthly or so, and that doesn't always coincide with the first day of the month. Be patient and give it time. As long as you stay diligent, your sites will climb in the rankings slowly and surely.

It's the job of search engines to find sites that match the criteria which people are looking for. Ultimately it's best if search engines list your site as a place of interest for anyone using search terms related to your subjects of interest. To begin, you'll almost surely start out deep in their results, like on page 20, but over time you'll climb ever closer to the top if you adhere to the advice that follows. Back in 2008 when I finally got serious about establishing an internet presence and searched via Google for my own name, I came up on page 17 or so and felt discouraged by that. In time I slowly climbed closer to page one even though my name is very common with over 700 people named Jason Matthews in the USA alone. Now my sites experience good search results for not only my name but for my subjects of interest (which is far more important).

Although in a funny way, you don't need to worry about the search engines finding your website. They will find it; I guarantee that. To know immediately if they've found you or not, simply type in the URL into the search box as in http://example.yola.com and see if it comes up at the top of the list. If it's not there, have no fear. It usually takes about a week or so before they index your site. Give it some time and try again. I'll instruct how to submit your sites directly to Google and many other search engines, but even if you don't they will still find you. How do I know this? I know because Google Alerts is set up to notify me on subjects like my name, my books, my download pages, etc, whenever anybody on Earth posts something on those items. It doesn't seem to matter how trivial or tiny the posting or the website is; like the concept of George Orwell's Big Brother, Google knows what's happening in Cyberworld.

However, you absolutely do want to maximize the recognition of search engines like Google, Yahoo and Bing **to not only find you but to associate the site with what you're trying to accomplish.** That means not only does Google see your site specializing in exotic fish, for example, but that it believes you really know everything there is to know about the exotic fish business because of the factors Google considers important. There are many ways to help in this regard, **but remember that this takes time.** Search engine indexes place value on how long a site has been in existence, and they prefer established sites with lots of data, incoming links and recorded visits over newer ones. Be patient and give it time as in months or (sadly) even years. Many of my sites have excellent SEO factors working for them, but the fact that they're less than a year old still counts against me. As long as you stay diligent with the advice that follows, your sites will climb in the rankings slowly and surely.

Keywords.

If you haven't already read the chapter on Deciding on a Domain Name, you might want to go back and read that now. Otherwise, I will be repeating myself a bit here because this is such important information.

It's my belief that **_keywords are essential_** to help search engines link you and your book to certain words, terms or phrases. It's best to add keywords to every site, blog and location that has boxes for them, keywords that describe the content of what your book is about. For example, let's say it's about having an elephant as a pet. You were gifted a young elephant and raised it to adulthood, becoming best friends with the elephant along the way. People were fascinated by the story and so you've written an ebook, created a blog and website, and now you're searching for the best keywords to market this. Keywords for this subject might include: elephant, domestic elephant, exotic pets, my elephant, zoo animal pets, unusual pets, training elephants, raising elephants, raising unusual pets and so on.

But there's no need to rush into things blindly when it comes to keywords. You'll benefit tremendously from a little research. For example, if someone Googles the word "elephant," their search will yield about 48 million results (Jan. 2012). Further research will indicate this term gets searched via Google about 11 million times a month and has low competition from others advertising this term as a keyword. The chance that your ebook will be anywhere on the first page is astronomically unlikely if "elephant" is your main keyword, even with low competition due to the other numbers.

Let's try "domestic elephant." That search term yields 40 million results although only 390 people per month actually input this term on a Google search, so it's not as large of an audience as you'd like. "Raising a domestic elephant" yields about 22 million results, but unfortunately almost nobody types that phrase into a keyword search so that won't do you much good. Let's analyze "exotic pets." That yields about 7 million results, has low competition from other advertisers and has a monthly average of

165,000 people entering the phrase. The exact term has less relevance than "elephant" but at least it has low competition and a lot of people search that term each month.

This is valuable information, right? How do I know these things? Because Google has a very helpful keyword optimization tool at this link - https://adwords.google.com/select/KeywordToolExternal. There you can type in certain words or phrases and get results on how many times per month Google actually receives that exact request for information. You'll also see a bar graph which indicates how much competition there is using those same keywords. *Ideally, you can find some keywords that have low competition from other advertisers and high numbers of searches from users each month.*

So let's go back to our elephant story and try to identify the best keywords. I'll input several phrases and see what comes from that. Let's try these: "exotic pets," "elephant," "my elephant" and "pet elephant." Fortunately this program will also show of bunch of related terms, so I don't have to list every conceivable way of putting this. You can also filter the results for unwanted words and include or disallow synonyms.

For our example (Jan. 2012), the phrase "pet elephant" yielded about 6,600 search results per month which is a good number, plus it had average or medium competition which is better than high competition. Even better, "my elephant" had 22,200 searches per month and low competition. "Exotic pets" and "elephant" had extremely high numbers of searches, but I just don't feel those are specific enough. Other phrases that showed and looked promising in terms of searches per month and average to low competition were: "buy elephant" and "baby elephant." Of course, this is perhaps a limited topic compared to another example like writing a book about overcoming an addiction or something, but hopefully the case is made. (Also these numbers constantly fluctuate, so when you research these terms it could be substantially different.)

For our example, I would recommend the keywords in this order: "my elephant," "pet elephant," "exotic pets," "baby elephant," and then your name. I would not recommend terms like "domestic elephant" or "raising an elephant" because our research shows almost nobody is using those terms in a search engine. Good research really helps. I use this tool before every blog post or writing anything important online that should be there for a long time.

Here's the link again to optimize your selection for keywords that will get better results - https://adwords.google.com/select/KeywordToolExternal.

Categories, Labels and Tags.

This is similar to keywords. Whenever boxes exist where you can enter categories, labels, tags, etc, think of them as keywords that will help identify you and the subjects of your ebook. Categories are typically more general while labels and tags are more specific. Keep these entries to single words or just a few words, not long-winded phrases. Also think of it as opportunities to mention your ebook, the subjects and your name that will assist search engines and others to identify you. Remember that Amazon, Smashwords and many other retailers also have boxes for tags, which help book buyers find what they're looking for.

Links.

The more links connected to your blog and website, the better. Whenever the opportunity presents itself to leave your URL link somewhere else; do it. The smartest way is to load your site in another browser tab and copy the web address, then paste it so you don't misspell something. (It amazes me how often people do that.) This simple act gives other people a chance to visit your site. Plus search engines record these links and each time someone clicks to one of your pages. Over time they start to recognize you're becoming more popular. Make it a habit to spread your links out to anywhere and everywhere possible, especially on all of the social media sites and places you've uploaded your book.

As I discussed before, *you can also leave comments on other people's blogs*, which is a great way to add input and leave your URL as most blogs that take comments will have a box for URLs. This is an excellent way to spread your URLs around since it's likely that people visiting the blog are also interested in the same subject. They might enjoy your comment and click to your site. Google Alerts will notify you of blogs on any subject, and within a few months you can drive literally hundreds to thousands of people to your sites by leaving smart and helpful blog comments.

Now, another tip is to click on those links back to your blog and website. Number one, it's smart to make sure the links work, and secondly those clicks will register with the search engines.

Add your URL's directly to search engines.

Even though there are hundreds of search engines, if you simply focus on Google and Bing you will be fine. In fact, you could probably only focus on Google and your SEO rankings could be terrific **over time,** but it still makes sense to do extras in this category.

There are several places where you can freely add your URL to their list. Here is the list of the best free places to add your URL for their directories:

http://www.google.com/addurl/ - submit your sites directly to Google.

http://www.bing.com/webmaster/SubmitSitePage.aspx   - submit your sites to Bing.

http://www.scrubtheweb.com/ - a great place to submit your sites to 10 search engines at once. This outfit also evaluates the effectiveness of your SEO strategies and provides recommendations such as "the Title should be less than 60 characters." Scrub The Web has been around since 1996 and has both free and paid services for helping anyone maximize their SEO performance.

http://www.webceo.com/ - this company claims to be the most complete SEO software package on the planet, and they may be right. It also has a free program to download containing in-depth website analysis and educational videos/literature. In fact, it has so much content and evaluations that it may be more than most people want to delve into. But the fact that this much assistance is free amazes me, and it certainly entices many customers to upgrade to their paid programs (although I think if anyone uses the free versions wisely along with the other advice I give here, they'll be just fine).

http://www.addurlfree.com/ - submits to multiple search engines simultaneously (up to 15 of them), but requires email and phone number so hopefully won't result in spam. They claim a great privacy policy, so should be okay. Consider this one optional (and the next).

http://www.searchengineoptimising.com/free-search-engine-submission - also submits to multiple engines simultaneously (they claim up to 100 but that seems like an exaggeration). In this case they ask for the return favor of adding their widget to the bottom of your webpage. It seems like a fair exchange, especially since the icon of the widget is very small and says SEO on it which looks sort of professional. As you can see at each of my ebooksuccess4free example sites for this book, I've added this widget at the page bottom in hope that it helps my sites climb in the rankings. The widget is a little black and white button that says, "SEO click here." See the example at my Webs.com site - ebooksuccess4free.webs.com.

Also remember back when you may have created a blog with Wordpress, they should have provided these links to verify it with the big 3 search engines here - http://en.support.wordpress.com/webmaster-tools/. This link is for verifying your site with Google and Bing search engines by adding metatags to your site that these search engines will eventually crawl and identify. Help with this can also be found through the Dashboard of your Wordpress blog, but you can also use this process at certain websites. If you scroll down the left side you'll eventually find a tab that says Tools. Click on it and scroll down to the Webmaster Verification Tools. There you will see the boxes that go hand in hand with the metatags you'll be asked to input by using the link above to visit the big search engines. And this will help too - http://en.support.wordpress.com/search-engines/. Now that you've created a website, you can use these tools again to further your SEO efforts.

If you build a site with Yola, they have an extremely easy to follow method for verifying with Google. Notice that Yola gives you both a Widgets and Properties tab on the right side of the screen. While the Widgets is fairly self-explanatory, the Properties tab is where you can add keywords and more to help search engines find and identify your subject matter. Yola has the Meta Tag Verification and you can easily followed the tutorials here - http://www.yola.com/tutorials/article/Tutorial-Google-Webmaster-1285944435809/Promotion%252C-SEO%252C-Traffic-and-Advertising.

With Yola and Wordpress, if you complete the verification process with Google, then Submitting a Sitemap is a simple extra step and something they recommend. Google says; *sitemaps are a way to tell Google about pages on your site we might not otherwise discover. In its simplest terms, a XML Sitemap—usually called Sitemap, with a capital S— is a list of the pages on your website. Creating and submitting a Sitemap helps make sure that Google knows about all the pages on your site, including URLs that may not be discoverable by Google's normal crawling process.*

This can be as easy as clicking on the Submit a Sitemap button and adding the suffix, /sitemap.xml to your Yola.com or Wordpress.com URL. Webs.com currently does not have the sitemap feature, but things may change so check back. However, you can easily verify each page individually if you want to be certain

Google knows more than just your homepage. *The HTML file is exactly the same for any page or any site that you create,* so just load the HTML file onto a page and verify it with Google. Once you understand the process it takes very little time.

With Webs.com, the Google Verification process is a little tricky but you can do it. Once you get to the Google Verification site - https://www.google.com/webmasters/tools/home?hl=en, click the Add a Site button and enter the URL of your Webs.com site. It will ask if you want to verify with a metatag or an html file. I chose the html file, which it then created for me and asked me to Download the html file. When you download it, Open it then Save it by choosing Save Page As a Web Page HTML file on your desktop or in your folder. Then I returned to Webs.com where I Single File Uploaded it to my File Manager (Browse your Desktop or folder for that Google file and make sure the entire suffix looks exactly the same as the link Google shows). Then I went to Edit my Homepage, scrolled to the bottom and typed in "Google" (any letters will do). I clicked to highlight the word "Google," then went to Link to Insert a Link, from My Files and chose the Google html file and Insert. Then I published the page and returned to Site Manager. Once this was done, I returned to the Google Verify page, where it asked me to Confirm a successful upload by visiting a site it highlighted. (This should take you to a dull webpage with Google and many numbers in the upper left corner. It should result in exactly the same thing if you click on your Home Page file link you just created over the word "Google." Test them side by side to see if they're **exactly** the same, if not try the process again.) Once I had visited the site in another window, I returned and clicked the Verify button and it worked instantly. I know this sounds complex, but if I can do it so can you.

There are many other sites that submit your URL to search engines. Because some of them charge money and/or require your permission for mailing list opt-ins, they don't seem worthwhile to

Preparing Your Website for Ebook Sales

This is cool. You're the writer, the publisher and the bookstore. There's no "middle man" in the equation because you are everything it takes to create, distribute and sell your product. That's neat, especially considering that this all for free. It only takes time and initiative. And to think this was impossible to do not that long ago.

It's true, in the beginning your website won't receive anywhere near the kind of traffic as Amazon or the other established retailers. (Actually it will never receive the traffic of Amazon, but as long as people are coming to browse your ebook alone, that won't matter.) Expect it be slow at first knowing things can change over time. The good news is your ebook is already for sale on the big sites like Amazon, Barnes & Noble and Smashwords plus their distribution partners so there isn't any dire rush to get them on your sites. But it's really the icing on the cake and a great place from which to sell. It looks professional and it feels good to see your ebook with a PayPal button on your own site. I currently sell a much smaller percentage of books directly from my sites as I do from the other retailers, but it all adds up.

When you begin it's possible that only a few dozen visitors will drop by in the first month or two. Maybe they'll buy your ebook, maybe they won't. That shouldn't discourage you if they don't. Everything takes time, and as long as you continue to follow these steps and take some of your own, you'll eventually sell ebooks. Hopefully people will like your book and recommend it. That's a big key to success in this business, positive referrals from readers. They act as a marketing force for you, so always treat readers with the utmost respect. You'll continue doing the things advised here like blogging regularly, commenting on other blogs and sending articles to online magazines and press releases (which we'll cover later). The next months you'll have more visitors and sales. Each month things can get better. Who knows? Maybe in a year or two you'll be selling thousands of ebooks from a myriad of locations including your own website! That's the dream, and I encourage you to dream it and to follow up with actions.

By now you hopefully have at least begun building your blog/website and likely know a lot more about website creation than before reading this. You should have learned or be learning now, how to upload photos, text documents, files and links to your sites, which is all it takes to insert cover images, ebooks and to enable sales.

But before discussing sales options, we're going to talk about three things: uploading files, samples and creating the Hidden Download page for the whole ebook.

Upload Files to your Website.

Before someone can download a purchased ebook from your website, you have to upload it so it's there. This is handled in the File Manager section, which is a pretty universal term so even if the site is not with Webs.com it should be called the same or similar. (On Yola and my paid hosting sites it's also called File Manager. On some others it's called Manage Files.)

On Webs.com after you Sign In and click Edit This Site, the File Manager is one of the main tabs. Open it, then choose Single File Uploader where you can Browse documents from anywhere on your computer and upload images, video and text files (like your ebook in multiple formats) onto your site. Once you click Upload File, it will upload and you'll see it listed there. You can edit a file, rename it, delete it if you're not using it later and want to conserve storage space. For the purposes of your ebook, the most important files to Upload are the ebook cover, the ebook in the big 3 formats (.pdf, .epub, .mobi) and optional plain text (.txt), plus you probably want a photo or more of you, your family or lifestyle for the About the Author page. All of these and anything else involved with presenting and selling from your website must be Uploaded to the File Manager first.

Samples.

I highly recommend uploading sample chapters from your ebook that browsers can click on to read for free. The sample should definitely include the first chapter or the first few chapters (combined into one) depending on their length. The reason is to give the reader a taste that hopefully hooks them on your story and secures an eventual sale. Since we already covered how to convert documents to multiple formats, you should make one or more chapters available in up to three different formats: .pdf, .epub and .mobi, though .pdf is the only mandatory format. Traffic that comes to your blog and website can click on a sample chapter, determine if they like the story and then decide to buy the ebook. Okay, how?

You probably have a Home page, an About the Author page and among others a page dedicated to the actual ebook. You can either add a Free Samples page or add it to your ebook's page. Let's return to the pet elephant example and pretend you have a page called, *Raising My Elephant*. On this page viewers can see a blurb about the book, the cover, a summary and maybe some testimonials. A sample chapter (or more) is usually helpful unless the book has major issues like typos, formatting, bad grammar, etc. These samples could be pasted right onto the page for simplicity, or they could be designed to be downloaded in different formats, which is something you'll have to learn anyway for the actual sale of an ebook. On a Webs.com site, *assuming you've already uploaded the files* into the File Manager for Sample Chapter 1 in .pdf, .epub and .mobi formats, then all you have to do is this:

Write something like, "Click the proper format to Download Chapter 1: PDF - EPUB - MOBI."

Then click/drag your mouse to highlight the PDF letters (for our example). Now PDF is highlighted.

Go to the tab that says Link (to insert a link).

Click on it and choose the My Files option.

Select the file for the PDF version of Chapter 1 and click Insert.

Publish the page.

When you View it, the PDF letters should be colored differently and with a click on it the PDF version of Sample Chapter 1 appears.

(Note that there is often an option when adding a link to have it pop up in a new window instead of replacing the one the customer was at. Whenever it's an option, I recommend choosing the new target window since it saves your original webpage on the customer's browser.)

Now do this for your other sample formats for however many chapters you give samples of, or you can just make one big sample chapter for simplicity. Always follow up with action by checking later that your links work as they should, that the files present themselves when the format is clicked on. Remember Calibre can be used to view any of these formats.

(Refer to the instructions above as the same way to Insert your ebook when we get to the Hidden Download page. And there you'll write something like, "Click the proper format to Download *Raising My Elephant*: PDF - EPUB - MOBI.")

Create a Hidden/Invisible Download Page.

(Note; I'm going to refer a lot to your "Hidden Download" page for the purposes of this lesson, but when you communicate with customers just call it the "Download" page.)

On most any website, pages can be made Visible or Hidden/Invisible. If a page is Hidden/Invisible, it won't display as a choice on the navigation bar, nor will it have a link to click so nobody will know it's there. From most Site Managers, this is accomplished with just a click to make it Invisible, as is Editing, Viewing, Renaming (something to remember for later) and Deleting.

The Hidden/Invisible Download page is where your ebooks can be available in all their formats for paid customers to download. They'll be redirected to it after purchase (which we'll explain with PayPal in just a bit), and expect to find themselves on the Download page to get their ebook.

To add your ebook to this Hidden Download page, just follow the same instructions I gave above for the sample chapters. Upload your entire ebook in multiple formats to the File Manager, then type on the Hidden Download Page which format people want to download, and then insert the corresponding file to the format spelled out in letters. Then Publish the page, check your work and make sure your ebook is ready to be downloaded by people who know where it is.

Some smart readers may be questioning, "But then can't they post the link for other people to go to the URL and get the book for free?" The answer is yes, they can. (Of course, they can also post your book on their own sites for free downloads, both of which can be fought with Google Alerts.)

And so to combat this possibility of your Hidden Download Page's URL being exposed, you'll need to check in on the stats from time to time. During my first two years of doing this I have only twice felt my book was being pirated. The simple fix was to Rename the Download Page and make the adjustment for PayPal and the StatCounter, which is also a snap and we'll get there in the Maintenance chapter. The original URL could be myelephant.webs.com/download.htm and (if you seriously believe pirating is happening) then with a simple Rename in Site Manager it could become myelephant.webs.com/k2zdownload.htm or anything else.

I've sold lots of books directly from my websites and can say this is not an issue. You won't ever have to make these changes until you suspect a lot more visitors during many consecutive days to the Download Page than actual paying customers. How will you know? If you've enabled the StatCounter on the download page (http://my.statcounter.com/) and restricted your own IP Address to not be counted, you'll know if the page is getting lots of visits without PayPal informing you of purchases. StatCounter works great for me, but it took about 24 hours to start registering. If you're having trouble using StatCounter, most websites have visible Hit Counter Widgets which you can install, or you can use Google Analytics for that page. The Webs.com Hit Counter (I believe) counts each one of your visits so keep that in consideration. There's also a better alternative at free e-zee internet for visible hit counters that work well. They are visible, which is why I prefer StatCounter, but they don't count you and can be set to count unique visitors and/or page views - http://www.e-zeeinternet.com/.

However, remember your customers are allowed to return and download in different formats. It's quite possible that only ethical, legitimate customers will have visited this page even though your stats indicate far more visits than purchases. Once I had 16 visits on a single day and only one sale. Instead of panicking, I simply watched the site for a few days and only saw visits that roughly matched sales numbers. Turned out the 16 visits was one legitimate person who just kept coming back. Personally, I wouldn't change the page title and corresponding info until I regularly had over twice or three times as many visitors as paying customers. Renaming the page and changing the corresponding info is quick and easy. We'll discuss exactly how to do that in the Maintenance chapter.

(Please note; obscurity, or no one reading your book, should be a much greater fear than a little piracy.)

I've made an example of a Hidden Download page for you to see. It contains three versions of the first chapter of my novel, *The Little Universe*. The example is to show some of the things you'll want to include and mention to help customers avoid any mistakes or confusion as to the whole process from clicking the links to enjoying your ebook. Please check out my example at this link - http://ebooksuccess4free.webs.com/exampledownloadpage.htm and feel free to use it as a template.

Selling Your Ebook from Your Websites

You have some options. I'm going to discuss a few: PayPal (PP), Ecwid, Google Checkout—which has merged with Google Wallet (GW) since November 2011, and a programmed data delivery like SmartDD that fights piracy with DRM. Two of these I'm barely touching on, one a fair bit while a huge amount of time will be for PayPal. My recommendations are for PayPal and Ecwid; either is fine. It's really a matter of preference so please read the entire chapter before selecting one. GW will just be mentioned briefly, while SmartDD will be in the Other Things You Can Do chapter.

(Side note; **my books almost never get pirated,** but many authors share concerns with me about piracy or others finding ways to get their product for free. This is a natural fear but not one to worry about too much. First of all, in a digital world there is always going to be some degree of piracy, nothing you can do to stop it entirely. *My advice is to keep the prices reasonable and happy customers will want to support you.* Most of the people pirating ebooks are targeting the expensive ones, those that are $20, $30, $50 or even more. Some ebooks are priced at over $100. No wonder people are ripping them off! Would you want to pay $100 or even

$25 for an electronic document? I'm not saying these ebook prices aren't justified by the value within; I'm just saying many people won't want to pay that. If your book needs to be that expensive, you can always email it to buyers after the purchase. Secondly, for most authors, if tons of people across the world were ripping off your ebook and sharing it because it was so fantastic—would that really be a problem? I'll argue that it wouldn't because more than anything you want to establish a reader base of people enjoying and referring it. And if thousands of people are ripping off your ebook and recommending it, then almost certainly thousands of others will buy it legally. *Perhaps the more people that rip it off, the more referrals to paying customers will happen!* Please don't get overly concerned about piracy. **Obscurity, or having no readers, is a far more legitimate fear.**)

(Side note continued; DRM stands for Digital Rights Management, an encryption code that Amazon and other technology retailers use to impose limitations and protect certain products from piracy and unauthorized use. It's a controversial thing and has plenty of opponents. Think of it this way; if you buy a paper book, you own it. You can lend it to multiple friends afterwards and even sell it to a used book store for some of your money back. Your one-time purchase went a long way. But if someone buys an ebook with DRM, she doesn't actually own it. She can't even give it to a friend later, and she can't sell it to a used ebook store. Additionally, DRM sometimes has issues with certain conversions and reading devices that can cause problems for customers to enjoy their purchase. Sometimes buyers cannot access their ebook, and they are typically restricted to one device to view it. Hackers have already figured out how to break into DRM encryption as well. My advice is not to worry about piracy or DRM. And if you do, then we'll discuss products like Smart DD later which might be a solution for you.)

What were we talking about? Oh yeah, payment options.

Google Wallet.

At the time of this writing, Google Checkout (GC) is merging into Google Wallet (GW) and still doesn't offer the flexibility or familiarity with customers as does PayPal (PP). Currently, PayPal is the superior choice in many ways. I'm not going to discuss how to set up a Google Checkout or Google Wallet account for these reasons:

GW currently only works with credit cards (Google Prepaid, Citi and MasterCard), while PP works with most any credit card and also with bank accounts.

GC holds money for two days, while PP's money transfer is fast.

GC interface for business is inferior to PP for things like sales records, transaction details, etc.

GC and GW are not set up for international currencies like PP is.

GC and GW have no live customer support, while PP does.

GW can't currently be used on eBay, should you eventually want to sell ebooks there too. (eBay owns PayPal.)

Because we love Google for most other things and since this may change in time, we'll keep an eye on GW. If you really want to, go ahead and offer Google Wallet as a second payment option though I strongly encourage you to offer PayPal as well. While it may be true that a few potential customers would prefer GW because they're more familiar with it, there's no need to set up your website's store based on the exception and not the rule. Since I'm going to spend so much time discussing PayPal, I'll leave it at that. The Google Wallet set-up will be very much the same plus they have loads of tutorials if you want to learn more.

http://www.google.com/wallet/

PayPal.

Most of the world is familiar with PayPal. This e-commerce giant has revolutionized the way many of us shop. I remember the first time I used PayPal around the year 2000, feeling a bit nervous making a credit card transaction over the internet. *"Is this safe?"* I wondered. Well, those days are long gone. Now I buy almost everything directly online if possible, and more often than not PayPal is the method of completing the transactions.

PayPal accounts can be funded by a credit card or a bank account. As the recipient of a transfer you can request a check from PayPal, establish your own PayPal deposit account or request a direct transfer to your bank account. Any of these options are okay in my opinion.

PayPal fees on ebook sales are fairly low. There's currently no added sales tax to worry about. PayPal takes about a 2.9% cut of any sale plus 30 cents per transaction. For example, if you sold an ebook for $5.95, you would make $5.48 after PayPal's cut. (Some may argue that a merchant account has a lower percentage of the cut, like around 2.3% with no transaction fee. However, merchant accounts have gateway and/or monthly fees, yearly fees and often sign up fees. If you do the math you'll discover it probably takes $50,000 or more in yearly sales before a merchant account makes more sense than a free PayPal account. If you're doing that much business, you can always upgrade to a merchant account later. For starting out, let's just stick with the free stuff.)

PayPal lets customers use the major credit cards, e-checks or their own PayPal accounts to buy your ebook. They make it easy to create Buy Now and Donate buttons that you can add to your sites very much like the widgets from before. They'll provide reports of all transactions and basically become an online bank for you with no need for credit application, set-up fees, monthly minimums, or any other hoops to jump through. They also pay quickly, transferring the funds from the customer to your account in little time. They claim to take security seriously, encrypting all of yours and the customer's information and preventing fraud.

That's not to say that fraud doesn't happen on PayPal. It's actually a constant discussion in the forums and a real bummer for many merchants. However, these people are usually selling tangible, physical products often to customers who receive the product and then claim that they didn't or the product wasn't as advertised. In many cases the dishonest customer gets to keep the product and have their money refunded. But that shouldn't be a problem with an ebook. If someone complains that they didn't get their ebook, you can say, "Fine, I'll send another right away. What email address should I send it to?" And sending another copy of the ebook won't cost you a thing but a few clicks of time.

How else can you protect yourself from fraud on PayPal? Probably the most credible way someone can claim their money back from an ebook sale is by saying that the ebook was not as advertised. It's important that you make it absolutely clear what your ebook is about, what formats are available and its length in word count. Here are some important tips from PayPal:

Tips for Safer Selling. - https://www.PayPal.com/us/cgi-bin/webscr?cmd=xpt/Marketing_CommandDriven/securitycenter/sell/TipsForSellers

1. Use overall precautions like **providing clear, detailed descriptions.** Buyers don't like surprises. Give a detailed description of your item and include photos or images where applicable. Images are especially important when selling in countries where buyers may not be as fluent with the language in which the seller wrote the listing. Let the customer know exactly what they can expect, how it's coming to them and what they should do in case anything goes wrong in the process (like the power cuts out during their download).

2. Respond promptly to any inquiries and issues. Show buyers you are listening with a prompt and courteous response to all questions. Work patiently and courteously to resolve any issues, even with customers who are behaving badly. You never know who that customer might be, and if they have a sour experience with you they might go out of their way to write bad reviews and

tell others to stay away from your ebook. Kindness just makes sense when dealing with customers on any level.

3. Chargebacks and reducing the likelihood of experiencing them - https://www.paypal.com/us/cgi-bin/webscr?cmd=xpt/Marketing/securitycenter/sell/Chargeback Guide1. Chargebacks occur when buyers ask their credit card company to reverse a transaction that has already been approved. Common reasons for chargebacks include:

Item not received. Buyer pays for an item but never receives it.

Item significantly different than expected.

Unauthorized use. A buyer's credit card number is stolen and used fraudulently.

If a chargeback has happened with an ebook, it's likely the formatting was poor or perhaps the customer decided they just didn't want it. You can do a few things here: either work with the customer to make sure they get a properly formatted ebook, or if they simply don't want it you should consider refunding their money. Sure, it may cost you 50 cents in the process but hopefully this will be the exception and not the rule.

Sign up with PayPal. You're going to need two accounts. The first will be for buying and selling products which is a Premier account. The second account will be a Personal account for buying only (testing) to make sure your buttons work before you go live. Since PayPal doesn't allow the same account holder to buy the product, the 2nd account is needed for testing. This is easy as long as you have a 2nd email and a 2nd money source like a credit card or savings/checking account that you can use, or you could always ask a friend to test it. Email accounts are free at Yahoo, Google and other places, so it makes sense to have more than one email especially for purposes like this. For testing you can also keep the price really low, like 1 cent which doesn't have a transaction fee, and then raise it to the actual price once you know it works. Remember to keep the details separate for your selling (Premier) account and your buying (Personal) account.

There are 2 main ways to enable a PayPal payment on your sites: Buy Now or Donate Buttons and Shopping Carts. I'm going to discuss Buy Now buttons because that is all most authors will need, and the set-up and implementation of a Shopping Cart is basically the same process. Even for authors that have more than one ebook to sell, by simply creating two or more Buy Now buttons, all of their needs are met. For example, on my main site I have Buy Now buttons for each of my ebooks individually and one button to buy both of the novels.

I'm about to give two descriptions of using PayPal Buy Now buttons; Method A is the built-in Web Store application on Webs.com or many other sites, and Method B is manually creating and implementing PayPal buttons that will work on any page of any site (including Webs.com). Method A, the Web Store built-in application is simpler to do, but it's inferior in how the checkout is handled plus it's not ideal for multiple ebooks. I recommend Method B (even for Webs.com and sites with premade PayPal buttons), but I need to explain them both so you can decide. In case you really want the simplicity of the built-in Web Store for selling one ebook (multiple formats is fine), I'll explain Method A first. If you have multiple products or want the checkout process streamlined, then Method B is the way to go.

Here's Method A, how PayPal works on the built-in Web Store application of Webs.com or similar site.

From the Site Manager, you can click Add an Application where you'll see extra features that can be applied to certain pages of your site. If you click on the one that says Web Store and then Manage App, you'll be prompted to enter Products for sale. (This by default will be labeled the Products page, but you can change it to Book Store or anything you want in the Site Manager with the Rename option.) There you can add the details of your ebook like the description, cover image, price etc. ***Remember to be thorough in the Description box to avoid customer***

112

complaints later. For the Product Image, that will be your cover which can either be uploaded directly from your computer or from your Webs.com File manager. Add the Price (\$.01 if you want to test it first with your 2nd PayPal account and then change the price once you've confirmed it works). Don't worry about Tax, Options, Shipping or Status. (You won't Upload your ebook here but just offer it for sale; remember the actual ebook in multiple formats will be on the Hidden Download Page.) And these items can be edited later so no need to fuss about perfection now.

Click Submit. You'll be directed back to the Products or Book Store page where you can see the new listing. Click on Settings. Check the PayPal box and fill in your associated ***sellers (Premier)*** email for PayPal. *Do not insert your 2nd (Personal) PayPal email for testing here!* In the Store Description box, make it absolutely clear what you're selling in terms of what the ebook is about, what the length is in word count and what formats customers will have access to. Your Store Policies should explain what they can expect; *that after purchase customers will receive a URL link to go and download their ebook in any format, that the link will work for multiple formats, and how to contact you directly with an email should they have any problems with the download.* Payment Instructions Field can be left blank or up to 40 characters explaining that credit cards or PayPal accounts work fine.

The Purchase Confirmation Message will be sent to customers after their purchase. Here you thank the customer and direct him/her to the Hidden Download Page (but don't call it that). Type out the URL address of the Hidden Download Page as well as insert a link so it is clickable. *This is an aspect of Method A that's not ideal, because you need to rely on the customer clicking a link in the confirmation message instead of automatically being sent to the Download page.* Explain again that they can download in multiple formats as many times as they want and how to contact you via email if anything goes wrong. Also explain that they can save the ebook format on their computer, where they can connect a USB or appropriate cable to download it to their e-reading device, and then they should use the safe-removal feature on their computer before unplugging their device. Also ask them please not to share the link with anyone else.

The Purchase Cancel Message is displayed to a customer that has an issue processing the order. Hopefully they haven't been charged, but if so PayPal will have information that you can check. In this box you should politely explain that you'll work as quickly as possible to settle any issues and leave your contact email so they can get in touch with you.

Unfortunately, only one confirmation message (which contains the Hidden Download Page) is designed to go out. *This is the other reason why Method A is not ideal if you have more than one ebook to sell, because you won't be able to send people to different download pages without giving them the link to both URLs in the one confirmation message.* You could rely on the honor system, but the real way to get around this (for those having more than one ebook) is to create separate PayPal buttons and separate corresponding Hidden Download pages which I'll explain next in Method B.

Here's Method B, how to set up PayPal buttons on other sites or even within a standard page on Webs.com.

Method B creates PayPal buttons that will work for any site: Wordpress, Blogger, Webs, Yola, Google Sites, etc. First we'll create PayPal Buttons before inserting them.

After logging in to your Premier account at PayPal and clicking either on Merchant Services or on Buy Now buttons, you'll be redirected to Create PayPal Payment Button. Then follow these steps:

Fill in the first box of Step 1 as a Product.

An ebook in multiple formats is still one product, so click the No, Create a Buy Now Button box.

Item Name can be your ebook title, plus I'd recommend adding (pdf, epub, mobi files) to it since customers will see that during their purchase. If you're offering more formats, list them here as well.

Item ID is optional and I leave this blank.

Enter the Price ($.01 for testing and you can always make changes later).

Customize Button (**I don't recommend this** because buyers are much more familiar with standard buttons, but I'll discuss it for those who want it). For an ebook you don't need the drop down options or the text field. You may want the customized button to look like the cover of your ebook. To do this, click to open the Customize Button option, then choose the Use Your Own Button Image. You'll be asked to input the URL of your ebook cover. This can be done if you have your ebook cover image on a website like Wordpress or Blogger (or if you use the http://www.docstoc.com/ program to create a URL of any image or document). If you use Wordpress or Blogger and have a blog entry with your cover as an inserted image, just go there and click on the cover of your ebook. It should come up as its own webpage with a URL in the browser. If you don't just make a blog entry and upload your cover image into the blog entry. Then update your blog, click on the image and you should have the URL for your cover's image. (Don't delete that post later though, because you'll delete the button's image.) Copy and Paste the URL and then input it into the box. (Sizing here may be a problem on certain sites, as it was for me on Webs.com. If you end up with a button that is enormous you'll need to play around with uploading smaller and smaller images to your blog or the docstop.com program until you get one that looks appropriately sized when it's converted to a button. If this turns into a drag, maybe just go with a standard Buy Now button.)

Shipping and Tax boxes can be left blank (unless the laws in your state clearly say you should add it. I'm no lawyer, just telling you what I've seen so far as I have yet to pay shipping or taxes on any ebook.)

Transactions Notifications can go to your email address.

Step 2 is good to have Save button at PayPal checked, but leave the Track Inventory and Profit/Loss boxes blank.

Step 3 Customize Advance Features is very important! *This is how we're going to direct people to your Hidden Download page after their purchase.* Check No, for customers changing order quantities. Check Yes, for customers can add special instructions in a message to you. Check No, for customer's shipping address. In the box that says, Take Customers to this URL when they cancel their checkout, check the box and input the URL address of your website bookstore so they can try again. *Here comes the really important part;* in the box that says, Take Customers to this URL when they Finish Checkout, check the box and input the URL address of your Hidden Download page. Make absolutely sure you did that so people will automatically be sent directly to the Download page to get their ebook after purchase. Make sense? *That's what makes your ebook business run on autopilot!*

Leave the Advanced Variables box unchecked.

Click Create Button.

Next it will take you to a page that says, "You are viewing your button code." Here you can copy the html code for a Website, and you can also copy the URL address for Email. Both of these are important, and you should copy and paste each of these individually and put them in your "ebooksuccess" folder and save them as PayPal buttons (one for Website, the other for Email). The Website html code can be used for Webs.com, Yola, Blogger and many other hosts. *Both the Website html and the Email code is what you'll need for a Wordpress blog,* as Wordpress does not support code for web forms or Javascript. For this reason, both Webs.com/Yola and Wordpress will have slightly different methods of inserting buttons, which we'll cover now.

Insert your button on Webs.com, Yola, Blogger, or any other website (not Wordpress yet) that supports web forms and Javascript. This is very easy, just like the badges and other html codes we've inserted before. In most cases they can go either in the body of a page or on the sidebar as a gadget/widget or even both. In Webs.com, edit a standard page for the sale and place your cursor where you want the PayPal button, click the HTML icon at the far right of the toolbar (or you can find that widget the long way through AddOns-Tools-Other Stuff-Your Custom HTML), paste the Website html code and Insert. Your PayPal widget should be in place, though you won't see it until you Publish or View. Also add some text near the button to demonstrate that it's the Buy Now button to buy your ebook and for what price. If you also want it on the sidebar, place your cursor over the sidebar in edit mode, Click to Manage Sidebar, select Custom Module, Title it "buy Raising My Elephant for $(your price)" or something to your liking and paste the html code in the Body box, click Save, Save Your Changes, Done, View or Publish and Publish all Pages. You can also go back to Manage the Sidebar to select if you want the widget on the Home Page and/or the other pages and where you want them in order. (For some reason, I had to do this twice to get it right, but there they are. Two PayPal buttons showed up after a retry.)

For Yola, Blogger or similar sites it's even simpler than what I just described; just add an html widget/gadget.

Follow up with action. It's smart to click on them; use your 2nd PayPal personal account and see if they work. This is also helpful to see the stats that PayPal provides on sales. You should have a functioning PayPal button.

(Note; I once got a call from a writer using these methods, but she couldn't get PayPal to automatically send buyers to her download page after purchases. We went through every line of the form trying to figure out what was happening. Turns out some people have to make an adjustment to their Auto Return Settings. I did not, as many people are set to default with Auto Return Settings "on." In her case it was set to "off." If this seems to be a problem, getting PayPal to send buyers to your download page from the Step 3 Customize Advance Features tab, go to PayPal and Log In.

Click on Profile.

Click on Website Payment Preferences.

Make Sure Auto Return is set to "on."

Even though I have multiple buttons, it has one button's return URL shown in the box. It doesn't seem to affect the other buttons, so not to worry if this isn't the URL you expect to see there.

Check and make sure it works.)

First I want to talk about Wordpress, and then we'll discuss changing your price from one penny to something else.

Now, let's talk about putting the same button into a Wordpress blog. Remember, Wordpress doesn't like forms or Javascript, so we have to use both the html and the Email code that you saved in Text documents in your folder. If you didn't save them, just return to PayPal, Merchant Services, My Saved Buttons, on that same button you just made click Action and View Code. Select and copy both the Website html and the Email tab and URL address (which you'll notice is a PayPal web address) and paste these codes individually into Text documents and put them in your "ebooksuccess" folder.

This link will help if you want to follow with pictures - http://en.support.wordpress.com/paypal/. (The Wordpress support tutorial uses a Donate button as their example, but it works the same with a Buy Now button.) Go to Wordpress and log in to your Dashboard. Scroll down the left and on Pages click Add New and call it "Bookstore" or something of your choosing. (If you want a choice of PayPal button images, you'll need to get another image's html code to display on your page. Get them here if you want - https://www.paypal.com/newlogobuttons, and click Download to get the button's html code, copy it and return to the

Add New Wordpress page.) Switch from Visual to the HTML editor and paste the button's Website html code into the text body. Switch back to Visual and you should see the button there (if not retrace your steps and try again). Now it's time to add the Link for the Email code into the image. Highlight the button's image, click Link and paste the Email URL code (from PayPal) into the URL Link box. Select it to open in a new target window if you prefer. That should do it. Preview or Publish the page and check that it's working.

You can also add a PayPal button into a Wordpress Image Widget for your Sidebar. Drag an Image Widget into your Sidebar and Title it, "buy Raising My Elephant for $(your price)." The Email code for the PayPal button will go in the lower box that says, Link URL (when the image is clicked). You'll have to insert a URL address of a PayPal button's image into the upper box that says, Image URL. Note that this will be an image, *something that ends in .gif or .jpeg for example*. Here's a nice one that I found in a Google search - http://www.lollipopanimation.com/images/secure-logos.gif. Try putting that in the Image URL box and the Email code in the Link URL box and see if that works. Remember, if the size isn't right just alter the Image widget's Width and Height with smaller numbers.

(Note; Dreamweaver and Frontpage users or anyone experiencing issues may need to check the PayPal Integrating Tips link.)

Remember to include the following instructions on your Hidden Download page: explain that they can save the ebook format on their computer, where they can connect a USB or appropriate cable to download it to their e-reading device, and then they should use the safe-removal feature on their computer before unplugging the device. Also ask them please not to share the link with anyone else.

And that should do it. You can insert PayPal buttons on all of your sites, both on main pages and in sidebars. After testing, remember to go back to PayPal and log in with your Premier account, Merchant Services, My Saved Buttons, Edit button and change prices from one penny to whatever you want and Save changes. This will automatically apply when someone clicks the button, as you can see in a test. (Note; PayPal may log you out if you've been inactive for a few minutes as a precaution. Just log back in to continue working.)

Hopefully soon, people will be buying your book directly from your sites, and the process will run on autopilot while you're sipping little umbrella drinks in Fiji (or perhaps sleeping at home).

http://www.paypal.com

Immediately respond to customers who bought your book from your sites.

This advice is so obvious it almost needs not to be mentioned, but **you should always respond directly to customers who just bought your ebook.** PayPal will send you a confirmation notice of any sale that includes the customer's name and email address. I recommend emailing them as soon as possible; thank them for the purchase, remind them of the download page's URL (in case something got messed up) and let them know you're available for comments/questions. You should also save their name and email addresses in a separate folder that designates them as readers/buyers of your book. This way you can contact the entire group later if there's an important news flash, sequel, etc. Of course, I do not recommend emailing frequently enough to be considered annoying, and always let them know they can unsubscribe to your mailings if they desire.

Developing and maintaining a relationship with your readers, even just a brief relationship, is extremely important to keep people genuinely interested in your happenings and for getting referrals from them to other potential readers. And because most people read books that have been recommended to them, this little step will go a long way with generating more readers from referrals. Plus it's nice making contacts with people from all over the world. I consider readers as friends, so maybe you will too.

Ecwid.

Ecwid is a shopping cart tool, which is an alternative to creating download pages and PayPal buttons. Some authors will certainly prefer this method. I have to admit, many will find it simpler overall and less likely to need occasional checks against piracy. As with using PayPal buttons, there is *no installation required* for Ecwid, unlike most other shopping cart options. I still prefer making custom PayPal buttons, but that could be based on familiarity.

Ecwid has free and paid versions ($17/month), though the free version should be fine for most authors. If you want password protected download links for ebooks, then that will require the paid version. Compare plans here - http://www.ecwid.com/compare-plans.html. Otherwise, the free plan works great.

Instead of creating a download page and directing a customer to it, Ecwid will host your ebook files and include its link in the reply email after purchase. After joining Ecwid for free, the process is basically this:

Log in to your Control Panel.

Choose Catalogue.

Click New Product.

Fill out the Name, Description, Price, and Upload an Image. Then Save.

Click on Files, Upload your ebook in PDF (for example), enter Description. Then Save.

If you have multiple books, they can either be in the same category (*ebooks* for example) or a separate category for each book as my example below will demonstrate.

I deleted all the sample products Ecwid provides (Fruits, etc) to keep the clutter down.

Go to Dashboard.

Choose between the html codes for the Product Browser Widget and/or the Bag Widget (which is useful for authors with multiple books) and/or the Categories Tabs Widget and/or the Categories Menu Widget. All of these can be used together or separately, depending on the look you prefer.

Copy the Product Browser Widget Code and paste it in html box or mode on your site, probably a blank page that will become your bookstore.

Follow their video tutorial for inserting the html code to your website at their home page. Notice the html code contains Javascript, so it won't be compatible with free Wordpress.com blogs. You'll probably need to play around with it a bit as I did to get it to look right.

I've made an example of using an Ecwid store at one of my websites. Yours may look much different as you can customize the appearance. Here's my Ecwid example - http://your-own-free-website.webs.com/ecwidstore.htm.

They also have a forum and knowledge base to help with any questions.

http://www.ecwid.com/

As with most everything in this book, there are alternatives to free shopping carts. Here are some more:

osCommerce   –   requires   installation. http://www.oscommerce.com/

Magento   –   requires   installation. http://www.magentocommerce.com/

Zen Cart – requires installation. http://www.zen-cart.com/

There are plenty of other free shopping carts, but from what I've seen Ecwid is tough to beat. However, creating your own

PayPal buttons that lead customers to download pages is always a free and easy option too, one that I've had success with. If you're not sure which to choose, you can implement both to get an idea of which selling method works better.

Next we're going to cover extra methods to bring publicity to yourself, your sites and your ebook.

PR (Public Relations)

What do you do once everything's in place? That's the time to lean back and watch the orders start rolling in, right? Wrong. Marketing books is about patience, persistence and determination. These things take time, especially with fiction since it's a luxury item. People buy non-fiction more often because they need to learn something, like the subjects of this *How To* book. But since fiction is pleasure reading, if you're marketing novels (like I am), be prepared to put in extra devotion.

The good news is that these things don't have to take much time. You're in the homestretch and just need occasional persistence to keep the word out about your ebook. Eventually, assuming people like it, a buzz will generate from happy readers who will actually help you with the marketing by writing reviews and referring it to others.

The term, Indie authors, is becoming trendy as more and more readers want to experience the brightest new writers who haven't been discovered by traditional publishers or the mainstream public. While it's true that many Indie books are not good (to put it mildly), it's also true that there are diamonds in the rough just waiting to be found. Fortunately, there are many websites featuring these books, often promoting them without reading but based on the premise and perhaps some reviews. We'll discuss getting reviews next, but first I wanted to give a brief list of some sites that are continually looking for Indie books to promote. Just visit the sites to follow their prompts for contact and submissions. Remember, this is a partial list as new venues are popping up literally every day, so a Google search will reveal plenty more.

http://www.independentauthors.org/ or http://www.iauthors.org/ - online book source by authors for paperbacks, ebooks and novels.

https://sites.google.com/site/1500authors/home - for Indies to promote all genres.

http://www.efictionmag.com/ - the premier Indie fiction magazine.

http://www.pixelofink.com/ - for free and bargain Kindle and Nook books.

http://sciencefictionshowcase.blogspot.com/ - for Indie science fiction.

http://redmoonchronicle.blogspot.com/ - also for sci-fi, fantasy and creative minds.

http://www.writeandshare.co.uk/ - looking for writers and poets to share their work.

http://www.bookstackreviews.com/ - Indie fiction for Kindle.

http://www.thereadersguide.com/ - this one can be tough to get into since they prefer books with many reviews.

http://authorsonshow.com/ - showcasing new authors from around the world.

http://www.ccebooks.com/esite/ - promotes contemporary fiction and non-fiction.

http://www.biblioconnection.com/ - passion for books.

http://indiebooksblog.blogspot.com/ - we're all in it together.

http://paperbackdolls.com/ - sharing our passion for books with the world.

Remember to use Author Central division to help make the most of your experience there. Obviously, Amazon wants you to sell as many books as possible and will do whatever they can to help. https://authorcentral.amazon.com/gp/landing

Press releases.

Press releases are great to get the word out about you, links to your sites and your ebook. There are many companies that offer free press release services, and you can even submit a similar but slightly altered press release to a few different ones. I do not recommend copying and pasting the exact same press release to multiple venues, as that may come back to you unfavorably (but you can try it, just don't tell them I said to). The companies will each have more specifics on how to write and submit a professional press release. Some general things to remember are that these are not supposed to sound like promotions; they're meant to sound like news copy, what's happening and why it's interesting. Submitting a release that reads, "I just wrote an awesome book and everyone should read it because..." is not going to fly. Similar in rule to companies like Ezinearticles.com (see below), press releases should answer the questions of what, when, how and why this matters, and not be a big sales pitch.

Here are some companies that offer free versions of press releases:

PR.com

Free-press-release.com

1888pressrelease.com

PRlog.org

PRWeb.com

Write and Submit Articles.

If you can write a book, you can certainly craft short articles. These can be articles about you and your book, or they can be subjects within your book or just other subjects. Like press releases, submitting articles is a great way to get your name and URL links out there. Remember to be professional when writing

126

articles and have them polished and of quality content. Then submit your articles to anywhere you can for free. You can even submit the exact same article to multiple places, maybe with minor alterations to each in the title and the first sentence or paragraph to help distinguish them. Here are some great places, and again more can be found with a Google search:

http://www.goarticles.com/ - the self-proclaimed largest free content article directory. I really like them in that the articles post fairly quickly, usually within 48 hours, and they aren't too fussy with rules. They send a confirmation email once posted, as does Ezines and IdeaMarketers. To see examples of articles I've written for this service visit here - http://www.goarticles.com/cgi-bin/author.cgi?C=282217.

http://www.dropjack.com/ - a place for brief posts and links to your sites. They only take 2 to 5 sentences so it's more like writing a few headlines and buzzwords, but it still helps with SEO and traffic to your sites.

http://www.ezinearticles.com/ - expert authors sharing their articles. This site takes a bit longer and is much stricter on following all of their rules for accepting articles but is really a great place once you get the hang of it. Your article must sound unbiased and not promotional whatsoever (the real problem with many of my own submissions). If your articles are denied, which happened to me plenty of times, don't worry. They'll explain exactly why and let you make alterations until you get approved. To see examples of articles I've written for this service visit here - http://ezinearticles.com/?expert_bio=Jason_M_Matthews. Notice that just because there may be zero comments, that doesn't mean the articles haven't been viewed. They have been viewed, plenty of times, and likely some of those people have clicked on my links. Also remember that leaving quality comments and links to your URLs is smart when you read articles of interest.

http://www.ideamarketers.com/ - a great PR and content source. They have paid programs but the free version works well too.

These are just a few but plenty to get started with. One thing you'll discover is that your articles will get picked up by other online magazines and ran without your knowledge. This is terrific in that your URLs are getting distributed and inserted by other people, like someone else working for you for free.

http://technorati.com/ - this is my favorite place to submit articles, often posts that eventually end up on my blogs. They have a huge reader base and can really drive traffic to your websites. They are a selective outfit however, and you will have to go through the process of getting approved to write for them first. For those interested in writing for Technorati, see the instructions here - http://technorati.com/write-for-technorati/.

Reviews and Critiques

Reviews are (in my opinion) far more important than covers. Most people read books that were referred to them. When first starting out, it can be quite a task to accumulate reviews of your book. In fact, one of my recent titles has been out since Nov. 2010 with decent sales and currently has only one review. Yikes, maybe they don't like it! Great thing that it's selling, but I sure would love to see more reviews for *How to Make Your Own Free Website*.

Part of the reason is because I haven't been overly active seeking reviews as I prefer for them to come in on their own. This may be a lazy and stupid approach on my part; we'll see in time. However, you may want to make a real effort to generate reviews, and this is often easier said than done. Here are suggestions for getting the reviews ball rolling:

Ask friends to read and write one. Family can be risky, but you can ask them too just so long as it doesn't sound like Mom proudly gushing over her kid. Distant relatives with different last names are smarter to ask than close ones. It's likely some of these people have already read your book and would be happy to continue helping. ***Caution them not to write overly sweet and gushing reviews that might be met with skepticism from other readers.*** Nothing annoys an unhappy customer more than finding out a pack of misleading reviews were left by zealous friends and family. Ask them to be candid and encourage them to list items they didn't particular enjoy to keep it realistic. Tell them to leave any number of stars; it doesn't have to be a 5-star review. 3 and 4-star reviews are fine too.

Ask members of forums to write a review. Offer a free book in exchange or offer to give a review for another author as a fair trade. Amazon Kindle discussion groups do this frequently as well as forums like http://indiespot.myfreeforum.org/.

Dan Poynter of ParaPublishing has a newsletter with a monthly reviews wanted section. It's how I got many reviews that ended up on my website for this very book. Just sign up for the free newsletter and follow the submission advice at http://parapublishing.com/sites/para/.

There are plenty of people that can be found with a Google and forum search. Some charge money, some don't. Many have a long waiting list while others might be available right away. Because this field is constantly in flux, you'll need to do some searching. A member of Red Adept's staff at http://redadeptreviews.com/ did a review of *The Little Universe*, but I had to apply for it and the posting came out 6 months later.

Google searches will reveal places like these:

http://www.selfpublishingreview.com/ - the name says it all.

http://authorjess.blogspot.com/

http://wordsmithpages.com/Home_Sally.php

http://booksbyessie.blogspot.com/

http://reelswellblog.com/

Make a mention to readers at the end of your book that *it would be greatly appreciated if they would be so kind as to leave an honest review.* Let people know it's okay to include elements they didn't like as well as those they did. In fact, I encourage readers to do the same for this book at Amazon, Barnes & Noble or anywhere else for either the ebook or paperback version. And if you didn't like it, that's okay too. I am sorry if that's the case, but not everyone will like the same book.

(Side note; if any customer would also like a free pdf version that might be handier on her/his computer with all the hyperlinks, just let me know. I don't have any way of verifying who bought the book through a retailer other than if she/he left a review, so if that sounds fair just direct me to the review and receive a free pdf copy. Email jason@thelittleuniverse.com with *free pdf for my review* in the subject box.)

Now comes the scary part. What if a lot of readers have complaints or simply don't like it? Maybe they mention poor formatting, errors with grammar and typos, or that the story just didn't work for them. Unfortunately, it's happened to me plenty of times. I can report with good conscience that not everyone likes my books and that's okay. This will possibly be the case for you too.

However, there is a beautiful thing about ebooks that's not true with traditional paper books. Ebooks can be regularly edited and updated. If a dozen typos are discovered by you (or readers), then those can be fixed and updated immediately. Amazon usually takes about 2 days to publish a newer version, Smashwords sometimes a week or more, and these updates can happen as many times as you want.

Content of the story and other narrative issues can be harder to work out. For authors who sense that the book simply needs to be better, it will probably be wise to join some writing critique groups and work on improvements. I mentioned earlier a few forums for writers which is a good place to start, and there are plenty more with a Google search for "writing critique groups."

http://indiespot.myfreeforum.org/ - a place for readers and authors to connect.

http://www.goodreads.com/ - all about books.

http://redroom.com/ - where the writers are.

http://www.authonomy.com/ - where writers become authors and more.

Affiliate Marketing

Who are my affiliates? Just a few little outfits called Amazon, Apple, Barnes & Noble, Smashwords and Google. Some of them, Amazon for example, make it possible for others to enlist my books on their sites and receive a small cut of any sale, so this field is growing everyday. But that's not what most people think of when they talk about affiliate marketing; they think of places like Clickbank.

In all honesty I am not that experienced with this subject because the above affiliates work great for me. I've looked briefly into affiliate marketing opportunities with the thought that maybe other people can sell my ebooks and turn a commission while I earn more money by having a sales force in my corner. I have not currently gone there but might consider it. (One thing that keeps me away is worrying about updating the books, something I regularly do, and having to track down affiliates with those updates.) Even though my experience here is limited, I've learned a few things and have opinions on the subject.

With affiliate marketing there are publishers and advertisers. Publishers, also called vendors, provide the inventory or the actual products for sale. If you have an ebook to sell, then you could be a publisher and that would be your inventory. Advertisers, also called affiliates, sell products provided by publishers. Advertisers may sell one to dozens or even hundreds of products, and they make a commission on each sale anywhere from 1% to 75%. Becoming an advertiser is typically free, while becoming a publisher often costs money. The system is designed to run automatically with payments being made to both publishers and advertisers through the affiliate company. This is clearly a win-win-win situation in theory. The content provider gets a potential army of people selling their goods. The salesperson can pick and choose which products to sell and get a healthy commission just by placing ads on their site. The affiliate company makes a bit on each sale.

At this point in time Clickbank is the primary name when it comes to affiliate marketing. To become a publisher, or vendor, with Clickbank there is a one-time $50 sign-up fee. I don't understand why since they make a commission on every sale, yet there it is, $50 more for them just to sign up. It is also necessary to have a website with paid hosting and domain registration, not a free site like at Webs.com, so these two reasons technically push Clickbank and most other affiliate programs into the Cheating With Money chapter.

The concept of having many people selling your ebook is certainly alluring. It's fun to imagine a hundred salespeople promoting your ebook and being amazingly good at what they do. In actuality, most of those salespeople may never sell a single book for you, as they likely have dozens of products listed with no preference for yours and they might not be efficient sellers. It's my opinion that if your ebook is going to sell effectively via an affiliate sales force, it must also sell effectively by you via the methods described in this book. *Ultimately my advice on affiliate marketing is to look into it as a way of increasing your existing sales rather than getting your feet wet.* Again, I apologize for not being more experienced on this subject so maybe I will have more on this in the future.

That being said, Google Affiliate Network is a free possibility for those with a blog at Blogger or a Yola site or other site that accepts AdSense. I believe this might be the only current way to accomplish affiliate marketing and free hosting in one tidy package.

The affiliate program through Google is free for both advertisers and producers though it will not work on certain sites like a free Wordpress blog or Webs.com site, etc that already have paid ads. However, it will work with Blogger since it's run by Google or at Yola. To begin you must sign up for their AdSense program as well as complete an application and be approved.

Other Things You Can Do

Publish paperbacks with CreateSpace. CreateSpace is Amazon's free Print on Demand (POD) publishing company. They have a number of programs, both paid services with help for any publishing need or a completely free design for do-it-yourself types like me. POD presses only make copies of the book as they're ordered so there's no need for huge print runs leaving boxes of books filling up your closets or garage. In fact, you don't ever have to order copies if you don't want to; customers can directly order via CreateSpace and Amazon, receive their books and you'll get a handy check in the mail at the end of the month. In my experiences it's been a very nice deal, as I have 5 titles set up this way.

For do-it-yourselfers, CreateSpace will walk you through the process of creating physical copies of your book with no set-up fees. Although I prefer to spend a bit extra for the Pro Plan at $39, which has major benefits including better royalty percentages on sales. They'll also provide a free Amazon ISBN if you need one. They have cover design tools for basic options without a lot of choices, or you can create and upload your own. You'll need to add a spine and back cover design as well and put them all together in one package, or just make one with their templates. A bonus is that CreateSpace is owned by Amazon, which gives you an Amazon webpage listing right off the bat. CreateSpace has a non-exclusive contractual agreement, so you're still free to pursue other publishing options. I've printed this and other books with CreateSpace, so look for it there if you want a physical copy or as a gift for a friend. (See how this marketing thing is ongoing?) They also have a huge support forum of authors for any advice on getting it done - https://www.createspace.com/en/community/index.jspa.

If you really want books in print and want the set-up free or very cheap, then CreateSpace is a fine solution.

https://www.createspace.com/

http://www.lulu.com/ - another do-it-yourself publishing solution for paperbacks.

Start using a hash-tag on Twitter for your book.

This may only work if a book becomes quite popular (like #twilight), and certainly it would take time. You could have a personalized hash-tag in your tweets that accompanies other hash-tags for more popular terms. Eventually, this could catch on with readers. For this book, I could use #HTMMASEBAFF. Since no one is currently using this hash-tag, I would have to include others to be seen on Twitter, like #Indie #author #writers, but eventually it could be this book's personalized hash-tag and something you could also do with your books. For an experiment type in #HTMMASEBAFF to a Twitter search box and see if anyone other than me has made an entry. (My 1st mention was April 13th of 2011, so we can all see if this sinks or swims. It will probably sink, but hey, the only way to find out is to try.)

Join tagging parties.

Tagging parties? Yeah, sounds like fun. Tagging parties are when groups of people (usually authors though friends and family can help) agree to add tags to everyone's books. Tags to describe and categorize books are primarily on Amazon, but other retailers might add this to their book descriptions. Tags are typically of the genre, subject matter, author and elements specific to the book. For example, tags of this book on Amazon include: self-publishing, ebook, writers, online marketing, kindle, epublishing, etc. Parties of people who agree to reciprocate can help accumulate more book tags very quickly and thus assist with in-house searches.

Do these tags have that much effect on sales? I'm not convinced they do and there's not much data either way. Some readers have confirmed to me that they use tags to search for books while others think they are unreliable for reasons like tagging parties. I've seen best-selling books with virtually no tags and books with lots of tags that don't sell well. Just in case, I've joined several tagging threads in hopes that it really does help. Sorry I don't have a clearer answer, but for now it's one of those extra things you can try for fun. Plus it's a great way to network with other authors, which might be the best benefit of all. You can find tagging threads at many writing forums including Goodreads, Facebook, Authonomy and more. Since June of 2011, Amazon has announced tagging parties and threads can be considered abusive to what the system was designed for, so if you participate in this it will have to be done covertly. Due to this announcement, tagging threads may become obsolete in the future at many forums.

Sell with Payvment on Facebook.

Payvment is an application for creating a Storefront on Facebook and elsewhere that will have a Shop Now tab where you can list and sell ebooks. Although Facebook is, in my opinion, one of the most important social media sites to make your presence felt, Payvment doesn't currently seem to be an effective method for businesses to make sales. This could change, but at present time most Facebook users seem more preoccupied with free social networking than for purchasing products.

That said, I still subscribe to the theory that authors should sell ebooks anywhere and everywhere they can for free, so I include Payvment as an option although I have only sold one ebook so far this way. I also don't like the extreme difficulty of setting up the store to run on autopilot. Selling this way is very much like an eBay listing, where you have to contact the buyer and arrange the transaction in the event of a sale.

Follow the tutorial on setting up a Storefront as it is very similar to everything else at Facebook.

http://www.payvment.com/

Google Alerts.

I'm repeating myself in case anyone hasn't caught on that this is a mandatory social media tool for finding blogs or mentions that can help you in multiple ways. Google Alerts is a neat way to be made aware when anyone online is saying something about you (or any subject you enter in the field, like your Hidden Download URL). Simply go to the site and enter the search terms that you'd like to monitor and your email for the results to be sent to. For the latest updates about you, your ebook or subjects of interest, enter different search terms for your name, the ebook title and subjects of interest.

However, you'll also end up with many notifications that are not about you but are the same words used in a different way, like if someone wrote a blog post that had randomly within it the words, "raising," "my" and "elephant," that would not be a direct mention of the ebook, *Raising My Elephant*. It can also be a problem if your name is extremely common. Even my name, Jason Matthews, tends to give me plenty of Google Alerts for other people with the same name or alerts that have both words, "Jason" and "Matthews" scattered in the same post. Ultimately I don't mind throwing out the trash notifications because it's really nice to get the ones that are about me and my books. If your name is Lisa Johnson or that common, you might not want an alert for this.

Sometimes you'll get an alert for a link to your ebook. It will have a clickable link so you can go investigate what this stranger is saying about or doing with your ebook. Maybe they've just written a nice review for you, in which case you can thank them personally. Or maybe they're posting your ebook for free, in which case you can contact them and politely request they put a stop to it.

So even though Google Alerts will often notify you of things that have nothing to do with you, sometimes the information will and that's a valuable tool. Give it a try and play around with it. It's fun and free, of course.

http://www.google.com/alerts

Host or Guest an Internet Radio Show.

There are sites where you can create an internet radio show or be the guest on someone else's program. Hosts are always looking for new subjects to discuss and people to interview. Authors and the subjects of their books are prime candidates to fill up air-time. You can also create your own show, interview others with similar interests and subject matter, and create a platform to market your ebook that way. Currently, few shows have a lot of listeners and many shows have none, but that depends on their marketing as well as the interest level in the subject. Stats of listeners to any show can always change quickly. Here are two free internet radio sites:

BlogTalkRadio.com
TalkShoe.com

For writers of non-fiction who teach something, consider creating a paid (or even free) course and uploading to a video training site like Udemy. It's an online tool for continued education where students come to learn, and instructors can design then upload courses utilizing Power Point, video, screen-casting, PDFs, audio, and zip files. Could authors of fiction use it? Perhaps. Some of their subjects (like Hobbies and Crafts) could be a fit to establish a video presence beyond a simple book trailer at YouTube.

The attractive thing about Udemy is that it offers a similar payment platform to content creators as many ebook retailers like

Amazon; free to join and upload courses while paying 70% of any sales to the author/producer. Courses can also be priced free, which might be a smart way to brand or network. The paid lectures typically range from $19 to $99 and more, some are even priced over $1,000. I've recently uploaded a 13 lecture, 7.5 hour video course for this book, which can be seen here - http://www.udemy.com/how-to-make-market-and-sell-ebooks-all-for-free/.

There are other venues for similar things including Sclipo, WizIQ, Myngle and Live Mocha.

http://www.udemy.com/

Free Auto Responder Email Forms.

Auto responders and subscribe forms are ways to acquire emails. If people visit your site and like what they see, they're possibly going to want updates. Your form can be simple yet should describe exactly what they can expect along with a guarantee from you not to share their information with anyone. You should also include a way for them to get removed from the email list should they decide to do so. Email lists of happy readers can be an invaluable tool, especially if you're a popular author and have dozens or hundreds or even thousands of readers awaiting news of your next book.

While the vast majority of Autoresponders are paid services, like Aweber, there are some for free that do the very most important part of the job, get email contacts for you. Here's a list of the few that I've found:

Responders.com - autoresponder and form for collecting information on your sites, comes with no ads. Request forms are easy to make with up to 10 questions that you can ask visitors. Easily integrates to a website with an html link. It doesn't create a contact list, though you can add emails of customers and those who express interest in an address folder. I also used this service as an example for this ebook. It seems to work pretty well.

Unfortunately, it doesn't come with a safe unsubscribe link, so you'll have to add a line that explains how people simply email back with "unsubscribe" in the subject field or the body.

FreeAutobot.com - autoresponder service lets you send out one or several follow-up messages at intervals you specify. No ads included in your outgoing messages. I tried this one out and wasn't very impressed, but it is free.

SendFree.com - autoresponder service with ads.

Remember to immediately respond to customers who bought your book from your sites.

A repeat from before, but this is important. **You should always respond directly to customers who just bought your ebook.** PayPal will send you a confirmation notice of any sale that includes the customer's name and email address. I recommend emailing them as soon as possible; thank them for the purchase, remind them of the download page's URL (in case something got messed up) and let them know you're available for comments/questions. You should also save their name and email addresses in a separate folder that designates them as readers/buyers of your book. This way you can contact the entire group later if there's an important news flash, sequel, etc. Of course, I do not recommend emailing frequently enough to be considered annoying, and always let them know they can unsubscribe to your mailings if they desire.

Developing and maintaining a relationship with your readers, even just a brief relationship, is extremely important to keep people genuinely interested in your happenings and for getting referrals from them to other potential readers. And because most people read books that have been recommended to them, this little step will go a long way with generating more readers from referrals.

SmartDD Secured Data Delivery.

This is *an option*, especially for those seriously concerned about piracy and DRM, as it's the most technically challenging thing to do so far in this entire book. There are three requirements for the software to work: your web space must be running at least PHP4, and have MySQL and also have the latest ionCube loaders installed. This is not going to happen on Webs.com, Yola, Wordpress.com, Blogger or some others, so it would have to be done either at a paid hosting company or at a site you've built from scratch. If you're fairly competent and tech savvy plus you want extra security on your sales, then you might consider it. You'll need to add software to your web server and fill in some ftp server information during the install which can be obtained from the host. There's an installation video to follow, but it's still a minor ordeal that left me with some issues to resolve with the company. SmartDD is a protected data delivery system that is about fighting piracy. I know, I've said not to worry about piracy, but the real reason I list Smart DD as an option is because some authors are still concerned and for its effectiveness at delivering the goods. With SmartDD, customers can click on a link to buy a product and receive it with excellent dependability. SmartDD generates its own PayPal button for your product and even emails customers directly after delivery and sale. And it's totally free for up to 5 products, or 5 ebooks, which would cover your 3 or 4 formats. (If you end up having more than 2 ebooks in multiple formats you could always purchase the upgrade.) You can also sell DVDs and CDs directly on eBay and have them created and shipped by Kunaki.com. There are affiliate sales opportunities and more; it almost sounds like one of those too good to be true deals, especially for free.

http://www.smartdd.com/special/

Resources.

Here's a small list of sites that have excellent forums and free advice to further your knowledge on some of these topics:

Maintenance

Back Up your Data.

There are some things to consider doing to keep your sites up to date and functioning safely. One thing is backing up your data and saving it on your computer and/or emailing it to yourself for storage. Fortunately Wordpress automatically backs up your content. From their support pages, http://en.support.wordpress.com/export/; *if your blog is hosted here at WordPress.com, we handle all necessary backups. If a very large meteor were to hit all the WordPress.com servers and destroy them beyond repair, all of your data would still be safe and we could have your blog online within a couple of days (after the meteor situation dies down, of course).*

But if you want to back up your blog content manually, you are free to do so by using the **Tools -> Export** *option described above (through your dashboard). This is still certainly a good idea, as if posts and pages are removed manually from an authorized user on your blog; there is no way to recover the posts. This will ONLY export your posts, pages, comments, categories and tags; uploads and images may need to be manually transferred to the new blog.*

For Blogger, click on Settings, Export Blog to backup all your posts and comments. To backup your Design/Template, go to Layout, EDIT HTML and click the Download link.

From Webs.com support; *we do not offer a way in which you can perform a "click button" backup of your site. However, we would never lose your files. The only manner in which your files are deleted is if you abandoned your site. In the event there is an issue caused by our servers we can always do a full restore.* Sounds like customer support can retrieve content although a user can't export files to their computer.

One thing that's pretty easy to do for Webs, Yola and others is to make a quick text document copy of each page. I just copy and paste the text from each page into a new text document, name it back up myelephant.webs.com and save it in my "ebooksuccess" folder. Only takes a few minutes. Just in case anything ever happens and I can't get my site restored properly, at least I won't have to retype all that text. The images are pretty easy to upload again.

Keeping an eye of your visitor stats for the Hidden Download page and the PayPal payments is also a main element of maintenance. If these numbers get out of whack over the course of several days, like three times as many visitors as payments, you might be experiencing people downloading your ebook for free. In this case, you'll want to create a brand new Hidden Download page by just Renaming it, simple as that. However, before you do that, if you have a Method A, Webs.com built-in Web Store, you'll want to change the PayPal button's confirmation message to go to the new URL link. If you have a Method B, manually created PayPal button, you'll want to change the part in Step 3 Customize Advance Features in the box that says, Take Customers to this URL when they Finish Checkout, check the box and input the URL address of your new Hidden Download page. Then Rename your Download page and check that your PayPal button works. Then go to StatCounter and Edit your project for the proper page to monitor and add the html code and widget for the new StatCounter button on the new Download page.

That should do it for unwanted downloads, and now only new customers will have the URL address of your Hidden Download page. In 18 months of selling ebooks, this has only happened to me twice. *Remember, if your ebook is being pirated by some, that's a good sign because it means people like it, want it and are referring it. It might even help your long-term sales!*

Addendum/Amendments/Additions

The bad news is it's nearly impossible to keep up will all the changes to the e-publishing industry. The good news for readers of this book is that I update this book between every 3 to 6 months because I want it to be as current as possible. Sometimes I learn of the changes myself, sometimes others inform me. Because of all these changes, an original idea from March of 2010 was to have an Addendum section for the book on my websites for readers to check for updates. This was in hindsight, not a good way to do it. Over time it became clear that the entire book would simply be updated regularly; thus the Addendum was never really needed.

However, you may want to check what's happened in the past years to see where some of the changes have occurred and were recorded. I'm no longer doing it but thought this brief evolution of the book was still worth mentioning. I also allow readers to contact me for more recent pdf versions at no charge, simply by mentioning that they have an older version and would like to check for updates. Again, if the book was bought at a retailer it helps confirm that by leaving a review at Amazon or elsewhere and emailing me at Jason@thelittleuniverse.com with the subject of the email *free pdf for my review*. See old Addendum entries at ebooksuccess4free.wordpress.com.

Review List of Highly Recommended Programs and Sites

YouTube.com - for tutorials on everything.

Facebook.com - best social media site.

Google Plus - other best social media site.

Twitter.com - unlimited potential for exposure.

Wordpress.com or Blogger.com- for blogs.

Webs.com - for websites.

Yola.com - for websites with no ad and good for Google AdSense.

StatCounter.com - for invisible hit counters, visitor data.

Docstoc.com - for creating URL addresses for documents and images.

Picasa.Google.com - photo enhancements.

Flickr.com – photos and Creative Commons.

Inkscape.org - cover design from scratch, image manipulation.

Smashwords.com - multiple format retailer/distributer.

Amazon.com - world's largest bookstore and great Kindle forum.

pdfonline.com/convert-pdf - converts documents and images to PDF.

2epub.com - converts Word (.doc not .docx) to epub, mobi, lrf and other formats.

Calibre-ebooks.com - multiple conversion tool and it checks your work as an e-reading device viewer.

Firefox - web browser.

PayPal - online banker for your ebook.

Ecwid – storefront for your sales.

PR.com - free press release company.

Goarticles.com - for submitting online articles and getting your link out.

IdeaMarketers.com - another place for online articles.

Technorati.com - for selective writers maximizing their articles.

CreateSpace - Amazon's free POD company if you really want some copies in print.

Google Alerts - if anyone online is talking about your ebook and for alerting you of important blogs to visit and post comments.

Organizations to Donate to Once You Can

Because many of these organizations are providing you, me and many others with free assistance, it's always smart to give back when you can. It doesn't have to be with money, but it can be with referrals and positive reviews. It can also be with money as I'm sure they'd appreciate it. Many of them have donation buttons and are even happy receiving a dollar for a cup of coffee. For the programs that I benefit the most from, it feels important to give back. Hopefully it not only helps the company but it helps other young authors or people in any field with their endeavors.

And so I encourage you to also give back when you can. It's good karma for everyone.

Cheating With Money

There may come a time where you'd like to spend money wisely to make some of these things better or add things that aren't available for free. I totally understand. With that in mind, as the epilogue to this ebook, I'd like to include a few things that I believe will make sense eventually to some authors.

Upgrading to a pure dot com without the extra suffix is a yearly charge of about $10.

Upgrading to ad-free hosting with more storage and bandwidth at hosts like Webs.com and Yola.com is about $5 a month in case your site develops substantial traffic.

Hiring a professional book cover designer could help immensely with sales. I was tempted to do this, but since everything I do in this book is by example, I did it myself for free. If you've seen my first book cover, the green one, versus the second cover, the one with a photo of me and e-reading devices, you'll probably agree that the second is better yet still not as good as a paid pro could do. The cost may range anywhere from under a hundred dollars to thousands so you'll want to take some time figuring this one out. Start at forums like CreateSpace and blogs like Smashwords to find reasonably priced designers. Cheap help can be found at Smashwords for both cover design and formatting by sending an email asking for these things to list@smashwords.com. Then Google some of the real pros who will definitely charge a lot more. Even though I believe the ultimate success of any book will be determined by the value inside it, I have to admit that many people do judge books by their covers. A good cover could start the sales coming in much faster than a poor cover. And yet, I've made a point to lead by example, to make my own covers for free, and even though they might be shoddy covers—I am selling ebooks. Will my covers win design awards? Of course not, but they will sell books as they already have. Hopefully they'll sell lots and lots of books and reinforce my belief that it's what you have between the covers that matters most.

Professional auto-responders like Aweber.com or GetResponse.com will be useful if your mailing list begins to grow beyond your comfort zone. They automatically update and manage your list, which will be helpful if you have several dozen or hundreds of happy readers.

eBay.com

There are low monthly fees for selling on eBay, but it can be a good option. I don't sell very many copies at eBay compared to my own sites or Amazon, but I do sell some. The thing I dislike most with eBay is that sales there are not an autopilot operation. After any sale I need to email the customer and give them the download link, which isn't a big deal but also isn't my preferred method.

You're not going to be uploading ebooks there, but you can make sales through the massive auctioneer. Selling ebooks on eBay is allowed provided that you're the author of the work or authorized to sell it as an affiliate. However, eBay has gone back and forth about their ebook policies. I don't know the whole history, but perhaps what kept the market open for ebooks was the physical CD. People would upload their ebooks in various formats to a CD and then sell that. How could eBay keep someone from doing that especially when so much music, movies and other electronic information was being sold that way?

If you search for ebooks on eBay, you'll find plenty on CDs as well as many in pdf and a few in other formats to be emailed to customers after purchase. The sales ad is usually accompanied by notes from the seller to the eBay staff and others informing that the ad complies with all eBay regulations such as: *I am the author or authorized to sell this work, it is not an illegal copy, no copyright laws have been infringed on, it does not infringe or break any rules set by eBay, Vero or the Downloadable Media Policy, and proof of these things can and will be provided upon request.* There are also plenty of warnings to the customer as to exactly what they're getting (especially if it's a pdf or other format) and how it can be read.

Just by researching what others are doing, you'd be wise to offer your eBook in multiple formats: .pdf, .epub and .mobi. The reason is because almost no eBay sellers are currently doing this, and you'd have that on the competition, offering your ebook to be readable by any e-reading device. It would make a great eye-catcher in your ad details and headline saying, "this ebook readable on all devices!"

To start selling on eBay visit the site and click the Sell tab, then Sell an Item. Follow the prompts.

http://www.ebay.com/

Using affiliate marketing companies to expand your sales force.

While I did mention Google Affiliates as a free possibility for those with Blogger blogs, there are plenty of affiliate marketing companies that have small one-time fees to list products including ebooks. You'll need a website with paid hosting to clear their approval process, but this could be a way to dramatically increase sales. Although it is my opinion that you must also be able to sell ebooks in the ways described here to have any chance at success with affiliate marketing.

You may want to hire out for all kinds of help related to your project with a company like oDesk, which enables you to hire people from all over the world. It's a free to join, online community of business owners and subcontractors who can connect and work together. Jobs can be large or small, full-time or just an hour. Many of these subcontractors are incredibly affordable for what they offer. Professionals in web development, software, multi-media, mobile web, sales & marketing, translation, administrative support, general office and much more can be listed for both job opportunities and employment wanted. oDesk takes a 10% cut on every job, so factor that into the equation if you're looking for work.

Here are some keywords many writers might use to find help at the site: editor, illustrator, designer, photoshop, graphic artist, e-book, copywriter, marketer, book cover design, logos, e-commerce, internet marketing, SEO and more. I personally haven't used oDesk, but my wife got some complex photo graphics assistance for an ebook cover for $20, which she was very happy with. (Notice she didn't even ask me first, but that's another story.)

https://www.odesk.com/

The End

Remember; if any customer of this book would also like a free pdf version that might be handier on her/his computer with all the hyperlinks, just let me know. I don't have any way of verifying who bought the book through a retailer other than if she/he left a review, so if that sounds fair just direct me to the review and receive a free pdf copy. Email jason@thelittleuniverse.com with *free pdf for my review* in the subject box. Even if you don't want the pdf, **it would be greatly appreciated if you would be so kind as to leave an honest review.**

That's it for now. I sincerely hope you'll put these elements into practice and find your time and effort rewarded with successful sales and a satisfying writing career. And I hope to see you at the Facebook group page for the title of this book - http://www.facebook.com/groups/110604178950149/. It's an active and helpful group of nice people, all trying to sell books.

Please remember, this is not a get-rich-quick scheme. It will take time. People read slowly. Search engines take months to really notice you. Being successful will require patience, persistence and perseverance to sell ebooks in amounts that make you happy. I hope you'll remember this whenever you're feeling frustrated by the process, *as I have felt many, many times.*

How will your ebooks do? Will they eventually become best-sellers? Maybe, maybe not. But at least you're putting the effort out there to share your work with the world. Will they have a profound effect on many happy readers who will tell you how much your book meant to them? Yes, that's very likely. It's a wonderful feeling and reward for any author to know that someone truly enjoyed his/her book. I pray this happens for everyone who puts the time and effort into not only writing a great book but marketing it in these and other ways.

Thanks again for reading. I wish you the best of success. Please contact me through the websites if you'd like or if you have further comments and questions.

Kind regards and best wishes,

-Jason

About the Author

Jason Matthews was born in North Carolina in 1967. He graduated from UNC-Chapel Hill in '90 with a degree in film and television. He lives in Truckee, California with his wife, Jana, and daughters, Shelby and Devan. They enjoy soccer, skiing, Texas Hold'em, and rooting for the Tarheels. He can be contacted through his websites, thelittleuniverse.com and ebooksuccess4free.webs.com. Visit his blog for regular updates on things related to e-publishing - http://ebooksuccess4free.wordpress.com/.

Other Books by Jason Matthews

These books are available as ebooks and paperbacks at major retailers.

The Little Universe - a novel about creating a universe and discovering the most wonderful things within it - thelittleuniverse.com.

Jim's Life - the sequel novel, about a teenage boy on trial who can see and heal the human light fields, being hailed a miracle healer as the world argues over his case - thelittleuniverse.com.

How to Make Your Own Free Website: And Your Free Blog Too - a how to book for building free websites/blogs and making the most with them - http://your-own-free-website.webs.com and http://your-own-free-website.com.

Get On Google Front Page - an entire book dedicated to SEO tips, written in January 2011 and updated regularly. I highly recommend this for rising in search engine rankings - http://getongooglefrontpage.webs.com/.

If you haven't already, please connect with me on:
Facebook - http://www.facebook.com/Jason.M.Matthews

Google Plus - http://gplus.to/JasonMatthews
Twitter - http://twitter.com/Jason_Matthews
LinkedIn   -   http://www.linkedin.com/pub/jason-matthews/7/122/435

Where applicable, it helps to send a personal note so I will know how you found me. Thanks.

Made in the USA
Lexington, KY
09 July 2012